JAGUAR XK8

The Complete Story

Titles in the Crowood AutoClassics Series

JAGUAR XK8

The Complete Story

Graham Robson

THE CROWOOD PRESS

First published in 2009 by
The Crowood Press Ltd
Ramsbury, Marlborough
Wiltshire SN8 2HR

www.crowood.com

This impression 2018

British Library Cataloguing-in-Publication Data
A catalogue record for this book is available from the British Library.

ISBN 978 1 84797 074 9

Typeset and designed by D & N Publishing
Lambourn Woodlands, Hungerford, Berkshire.

Printed and bound in India by Replika Press Pvt. Ltd.

Contents

Acknowledgements

As ever, I simply could not have assembled the facts, statistics and images for this book without consulting many other acknowledged Jaguar experts and historians. In particular I would like to relay my very grateful thanks to the following people:

Anders Clausager – who, as chief archivist of the Jaguar Daimler Heritage Trust, has so helpfully provided much knowledge and great enthusiasm. Production figures and other statistical information came from him and his colleagues.

Karam Ram – one of Anders' associates, who helped me locate some valuable historic images, both of the XK8 family and its predecessors.

John Blunsden – like me, a long-time motoring enthusiast, who helped and advised me on many Jaguar matters.

Mike Cook – who not only guided Jaguar's public affairs efforts in the USA for many years, but who now looks after all things historical at the

Jaguar HQ at Mahwah, New Jersey. Mike is also an accomplished author and researcher, who put me straight on several occasions.

Bob Dover – the man whose team developed the XK8/XKR, and who went on to be Jaguar's 'big boss' in later years; he also helped me with memories and guidance on this exciting period.

Trevor Crisp – whose team designed the fabulous AJ-V8 engine, and who spent a lot of time telling me how, when, and where that engine progressed from 'good idea' to triumphantly efficient and well loved production power unit.

Don Hume – director, Jaguar and Land Rover Corporate & Governmental Affairs, provided much invaluable information about later-model XKs, and about the new generation XK range.

Paul Skilleter – another Jaguar historian, researcher and writer, who makes all my efforts look puny and under-cooked.

Introduction

A few years ago I wrote a complete model history of the long-running Jaguar XJS: *Jaguar XJ-S – The Complete Story*. Once that book was published by The Crowood Press, we discovered that interest in Jaguar's big, smart, refined and extremely capable sporty machines was even higher than expected. I needed little encouragement, therefore, to write this companion volume to XJS – which is the story of the life and times of the smoothly styled XK8 and XKR models.

Although Ford's ownership of Jaguar has now ended, many enthusiasts forget just how important that period of twenty years was to the continuing survival of the marque. Without the financial backing, the marketing support and the sheer pride of ownership that Ford brought to Jaguar, I doubt if the company could possibly have survived the turbulent 1990s. In particular, I doubt if it would ever have been possible for the XK8 – the true and direct descendant to the XJS – to be put on sale.

As with the XJS, so with the XK8: Jaguar had to make a big choice. Should they try to bring a technically adventurous new model to market (think of the original E-Type, and you will see what I mean), or should they adopt the down-to-earth and practical approach of a car such as the XJS instead? At heart, almost everyone at Jaguar would have liked to repeat the *coup de théâtre* that gave birth to the E-Type in 1961, but almost everyone realized that this was never going to be practically possible.

Producing the XK8 (and the supercharged XKR that followed it) was a classic case of the 'art of the possible'. Here was a direct successor to the XJS, much smarter, much faster, much more practical, and with a magnificent new V8 power unit, which went on to be a great success. It looked better than the XJS, it fought all of its rivals at the same level (and out-ranked them in some ways), and somehow it had the timeless style that made many a Jaguar enthusiastic hark back to cars such as the E-Type, but equally, see how the modern was an all-round better car.

By any standards, the XK8 went on to be a commercial success, and should be remembered for that, for the generally high performance and comfort levels it provided, and how it paved the way for even higher-tech sporty Jaguars that followed in the early 2000s. I thoroughly enjoyed researching and assembling the information about the way the cars evolved and improved from 1996 to 2005 – and I hope you will like the result.

Graham Robson

Timeline

March 1993	Full preview of XJS-based Aston Martin DB7, giving valuable clues to the style and form of a new-generation sporting Jaguar. DB7 deliveries began in mid-1994.
Late 1995	Pilot production of XK8 models began. Twenty cars were produced before the end of the year.
January 1996	First details of all-new AJ-V8 engine were made public.
March 1996	First official preview of XK8 Coupé model at Geneva Motor Show. New model intended to replace long-running XJS range.
April 1996	First official preview of XK8 Convertible, at New York Motor Show. Final old-type XJS models produced at Browns Lane. Pre-production of new XK8 began.
October 1996	Sales of XK8 models began in all major markets, including the USA.
March 1998	Launch of XKR at Geneva Motor Show.
October 1998	Launch of XK180 project car, at the Paris Motor Show.
January 2000	Launch of the F-Type project car, at the Detroit Motor Show.
April 2000	Launch of XKR 'Silverstone' Limited Edition, only 100 to be made.
March 2002	Original release of 4.2-litre engine details.
September 2002	XK and XKR relaunched with 4.2-litre V8 engine and six-speed automatic transmission
December 2003	End of production of XJS-XK8-based Aston Martin DB7 family.
March 2004	Detail retouching of style/design/engineering.
January 2005	Launch of advanced lightweight coupé concept – actually a 'taster' for the new generation XK that would follow.
March 2005	Introduction of '4.2S' limited edition models, as final run-out models.
Summer/ autumn 2005	XK8 and XKR replaced by new-generation cars. Series production ended in late May.
Summer 2005	Closure of Browns Lane final assembly lines, where all XK8/XKR cars had been assembled since 1996. Future XK models would be assembled at Castle Bromwich, next to the body plant.

1 Ancestor – the XJ-S

We all have ancestors, and not just human beings and animals, but motor cars have them too. Whether we are tracing an entire nation's history, that of just one family, or that of a famous piece of machinery, we must usually look back some way, and some considerable time, to establish where the roots *really* were. Motoring historians, like archaeologists, must

Even though Jaguar's founder, Sir William Lyons, had officially retired from business in 1972, he made regular trips to Browns Lane while the XJ-S was a current product, and when first thoughts on the XJ41 were already forming.

sometimes dig back a long way in their search for true origins.

And so it was with Jaguar's XK8. Beautiful though it was, sleek though it undoubtedly was, and advanced though it was, when it was announced in 1996 it had not suddenly been plucked out of thin air, as the first of the line: as this book will make clear, it was more likely to be the last of the line.

Before the XK8 there was the Aston Martin DB7, before that there had been the still-born XJ41/XJ42 projects, before that there was the long-running Jaguar XJS, and before *that* there was the original Jaguar XJ6 saloon of 1968.

Still with me? For the fact is, that when surveying the XK8 we can certainly trace some technical lineage and basic engineering architecture back to the Jaguar XJ6 saloons of the late 1960s. To make this all crystal clear, the simplest possible summary I can make is that the story really began with the development of an all-new monocoque platform for the XJ6 saloon (and that really *was* new, and had been some time in the making), a design that would eventually prove to be ideal as the versatile base for many derivatives in the 1970s. Crucially, there would be longer-wheelbase and shorter-wheelbase derivatives.

One important off-shoot of that new platform, all-independent suspension and running gear, though in shorter-wheelbase form, formed the basis of the XJ-S, a sporty type which made its debut in 1975. The last of the XJ6-based saloons would not be made until 1997 (and that was actually a V12-engined car), which was a year after the XJS (the hyphen having disappeared meantime) had itself gone out of production. And, by that time, production of the XK8, which still owed much to the XJ6 saloons, had begun.

This, then, is a complex story whose philosophical origins were in the 1960s. That was the period in which Jaguar's founder, Sir William Lyons, began his search for one new range of cars to replace the mish-mash of differently styled saloons – Mark IIs, S-Types and 420s –

that were currently being produced at Browns Lane, Allesley, on the outskirts of Coventry. To replace three distinctly different body styles (original, long-tail, plus front-and-rear facelifts, which hid two types of rear suspension, and four different engine sizes), Sir William proposed one commodious new four-door saloon body shell, with a choice of 6-cylinder, V8-cylinder and V12-cylinder engines.

Workforce exiting Swallow Road Factory, Coventry, ca. 1936. This factory was bursting at the seams by 1950, and set William Lyons searching for more space.

The legendary XK120, introduced in 1948, was Jaguar's first post-war Roadster, and its DNA would be in every XJ-S, and later XK8, which followed on forty and fifty years later.

Sir William Lyons posed alongside the E-Type, which did so much to underpin Jaguar's fortunes in the 1960s and 1970s. It is easy to see where the inspiration for the sleek lines of the XK8 came from.

A very telling photograph, with one of (SS-) Jaguar's very earliest two-seaters, the red SS100, ahead of an XK8, showing how styling had changed in sixty years.

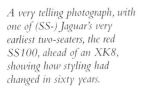

Browns Lane

Although all SS cars, SS-Jaguars and early post-war Jaguars were produced at a factory in Foleshill, in the northern suburbs of Coventry, this was bursting at the seams by 1950, and set William Lyons searching for more factory space. At this time the city was going through something of an industrial upheaval, because several of the original aero-engine 'shadow' factories that had provided so much invaluable military hardware during World War II were becoming redundant.

The government's 'shadow' factory scheme had been launched in 1936, to boost the aviation rearmament programme and to get the motor industry involved in setting up, running and managing new aero-engine factories. No sooner was the first wave of factories up and running, than the government initiated Phase Two, the result being that Daimler built and managed 'Shadow No. 2' in Browns Lane, Allesley, just a few miles to the west of Coventry. This building began by manufacturing Bristol Hercules radial engines during the war, but by the early 1950s it was closed down, Daimler having no further use for it.

William Lyons eventually bought the plant, began moving his assembly facilities into place during 1951, and completed the move during 1952. Once the move had been completed, Jaguar's original Foleshill factory was sold off to Dunlop. Browns Lane would then be the home of Jaguar until 2005 (when car assembly, and XK8 assembly, finally closed down), though it was modified, expanded, rejigged and persistently modernized many times in that period. The purchase of the Daimler business, and its factories in Radford, Coventry, and the opening up of the Jaguar technical centre at Whitley, Coventry, did not change that.

Every XK8, of whatever type, was completed at Browns Lane.

Even as recently as 1991, the city council opened a new road linking the Allesley by-pass to Brownshill Green, in which a major feature was a new roundabout, and gave direct access to the old 'back gate', now the official 'new' main entrance to Browns Lane.

Ford, which controlled Jaguar after 1989, immediately laid plans to invest in Browns Lane to produce ever more cars in the late 1990s and early 2000s. The first benefit came with approval to launch the much-revised XJS of 1991, then came the installation of new final assembly lines, while in 1996 the launch of the XJS's replacement, the XK8, was a further, major phase.

Four cars with the same pedigree – SS100, XK120, E-Type and XK8 – showing just how Jaguar's sporting heritage was preserved over the years.

When Jaguar introduced the sensational E-Type in 1961, it changed the face of Jaguar – for ever. The XJ-S, which took over in 1975, reverted to a much more conventional style.

The E-Type coupé of 1961 was the first sporting Jaguar to use a fastback/hatchback style. It was an inspiration for many Jaguars that followed.

With an all-new unit-construction body shell, and new 'chassis' platform, the XJ6 was first revealed in 1968. That same platform, shorter in the wheelbase, and somewhat modified, was used under the XJ-S and would also find a home under the XK8.

Not that it worked out quite like that – or at least, not in the originally planned time-scale. As with most Jaguar developments of the period, there were delays (sometimes to save money, and sometimes because of a distinct shortage of money!), which meant that in the beginning the original XJ6 would be revealed with two different types of old-style XK 6-cylinder engines, on a wheelbase of 108.75in/2,762mm, with wide tracks of 58in/1,473mm, and with the latest iteration of Jaguar's unique coil spring/independent rear suspension layout.

But that was just the start. In the next few years, the wheelbase of that platform would not only be stretched (to 112.75in/2,864mm for the saloons), but in due course it would also be shortened (to a mere 102in/2,591mm) for the sporting XJ-S. Not only that, but the long-awaited 5.3-litre V12 engine (which had been promised in 1968 when the pedigree was still new, but did not actually break cover until 1971) finally made its appearance – this actually being only the second all-new Jaguar engine to have been finalized since World War II had ended twenty-six years earlier.

XJ-S – First Thoughts

In the meantime, Jaguar continued to sell thousands of the sleek E-Type models – open top or hatchback types – every year, but by the early 1970s, once the new V12 engine had been grafted into the modified structure (with some difficulty, it has to be admitted), it was time for the planners to start looking around for a successor. It is no secret (see *Jaguar XJ-S: The Complete Story* for the details) that this process took ages, and that the XJ-S that finally went on sale in 1975 was not the car that had originally been schemed up: the car that went on sale was heavier, and not as sleekly styled as Jaguar had originally hoped.

Even so, there is no doubt that without the XJ-S there could never have been an XK8, so the origins and evolution of that car are very

important to our story. Project XJ27 began to take shape in 1970 and took five years to reach the assembly lines – it had had to take its place in the queue for development priorities, not only queuing behind the new V12-engined Series III E-Type, but behind the V12-engined XJ12 saloon as well. In the meantime, and right at the top of the management tree, Jaguar's founder, Sir William Lyons, decided to retire in 1972, handing over control at that time to 'Lofty' England, and this caused further delays and reappraisals.

This was a time when Jaguar's various 'XJ…' design studies came and went – they never progressed further than paper studies, styling studio models, or full-size mock-ups in wood and fibreglass – for at one time there was an XJ21 that might have been a direct E-Type replacement, and an XJ25 that soon matured into the Series III E-Type. XJ27 then followed on, as a car that could take over from the E-Type, but would not be based upon it – and this is where the XJ-S model was really born.

Right from the start, it seems, XJ27 was only considered as a closed coupé, and a 2+2 (really an 'almost four-seater') layout at that. In fairness, I should mention that there was also an XJ28 project code, which denoted an open-top version of XJ27, but little ever seems to have been done to turn this paper study into reality. Conversely, towards the end of the run, open-top E-Types were the only types that remained in production, because the fastback coupé/hatchback type had been dropped a year earlier. Even so, there appeared to be little pressure from dealerships to revive that layout. In any case, by the early 1970s there were mounting pressures in the USA from the automotive 'safety-at-all-costs' killjoy lobby, which strongly urged that all open-top cars should be banned.

Many years later, 'Lofty' England, who had retired by the time the XJ-S appeared, had this to say:

> One of the biggest failings of the E-Type was the fact that you hadn't got enough room in the

scuttle to get a decent air-conditioning set-up in there, which is pretty vital, and this is the reason why we went to the XJ-S…. If you're sitting in a traffic jam, you need some room to move, and you need a proper, decent air-conditioning system. The E-Type hadn't got it.

Not only that, but when the XJ27 project was on its way to maturity, there was never any doubt that it would be a V12-powered car, mainly with automatic transmission. The only alternative discussed was to use the legendary old 6-cylinder XK engine for an 'entry-level' model – but by that time, this engine was a

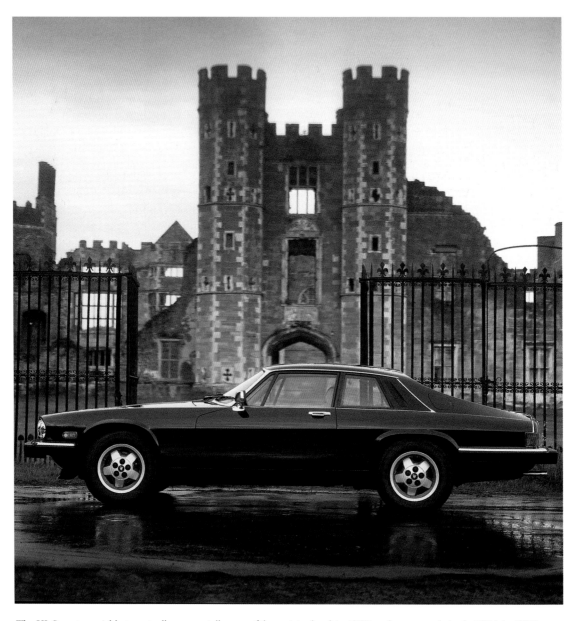

The XJ-S, controversial but eventually commercially successful, was introduced in 1975, and went on sale in the USA in 1976.

Although the Cabriolet layout was an attractive solution to keeping an open-top XJ-S body shell stiff enough, it did not sell in big numbers in the 1980s.

After much experimentation, and stiffening up of an open-top shell, the XJ-S Convertible went on sale in 1988.

The XJS was reshaped in the early 1990s, and looked like this until 1996, when it finally gave way to the new XK8.

quarter of a century old, heavy, reluctant to rev much above 5,000rpm, and was near the end of its development. Almost by default, therefore, XJ27 was beginning to take shape, with a massive V12 engine filling the available bonnet space, and with a bulky XJ6/XJ12 type of air conditioning designed as an integral part of the scuttle/instrument panel.

As ever, at Jaguar, work began on the exterior styling of the new vehicle before any significant detailed engineering, under the skin, ever took place. Although Sir William (who

was his own stylist) was easily persuaded that a shortened version of the XJ6/XJ12 saloon's platform and running gear should be used for XJ27, the big question at first was – how short? Studies were made of a car based on the standard XJ6's wheelbase of 108.75in/2,762mm, but since Jaguar was already planning to market a two-door version (a 'coupé') of the XJ6/XJ12 on that wheelbase, there seemed to be no point in duplicating it.

Instead, and even while styling work was proceeding, the wheelbase dimension was

This was the very first XJ-S advert placed by Jaguar in North America in 1976, when the company emphasized the move from the sinuous curves of the E-Type, which had been dropped, and the more craggy, but surprisingly wind-cheating XJ-S that took over from it.

ruthlessly pared down to 102in/2,591mm – which was, incidentally, no less than 9in/229mm *shorter* than that of the outgoing Series III E-Type. This time round, and because the XJ27 was set to be a lot wider than the E-Type had ever been, Jaguar was determined to make the interior package much more roomy than before, and to provide a really spacious luggage boot that would overhang the wheelbase at the rear by a large margin.

The shape of the new car, either in its original form, or as face-/tail-lifted in 1991, was always controversial. The general proportions were, of course, partly fixed by the wheelbase and the general layout of the platform and running gear, but the shape itself was totally different from that of the E-Type it was to replace, and of course used no carry-over panels from that car.

As with previous Jaguar cars, Sir William Lyons was much involved in the development of the shape of what became the XJ-S (though I must emphasize that he had had nothing to do with the form of the E-Type), but even when he retired from the business in March 1972, it had not been finalized. The most controversial

---

Castle Bromwich – the Body and Pressings Plant

Jaguar's Castle Bromwich body plant has had a complex history, yet was only dedicated to the building of Jaguar body shells from the early 1980s. By the end of the 1990s, though, it was much modernized and extended to accommodate new facilities for the complete manufacture and assembly of a new generation of smaller Jaguars – the S-Types.

Before the 1980s, Jaguar had never had a dedicated body supply plant of its own. Once the Mark VII had been launched in 1950, its saloon shells, and later its monocoques, were sourced from the Pressed Steel (later Pressed Steel Fisher) Co. Ltd factories at Cowley (near Oxford), and later from Swindon.

Although the Castle Bromwich factory is only 5 miles (8km) north-east of the centre of Birmingham, alongside the A452, and is very close to Junction 5 of the M6 motorway, the site overlooked green fields until the 1940s. The first buildings on this site were erected as a 'shadow' factory for military aircraft production. Building work began in 1938, and the plant was ready to start producing Spitfires in 1940, with the Nuffield Organisation managing the business. Then, after a blazing row between Lord Nuffield and the Minister for Aircraft Production, Lord Beaverbrook, the plant was re-allocated to Vickers Armstrong.

During World War II the plant expanded enormously, eventually building 12,000 Spitfires and 300 Lancasters, the area on the other side of the public road being Castle Bromwich airfield where all flight test operations took place. After the war this massive plant was then taken over by Fisher & Ludlow, which was then an independent motor car body-making concern.

A series of mergers then followed. F & L was absorbed by BMC (Austin, Morris and other satellite brands) in 1953, became a part of Pressed Steel Fisher in the 1960s, and after 1968 was soon almost submerged into the mass of British Leyland. Up to that time, the 'Fisher' factory had concentrated on building bodies and monocoques for BMC, including Minis, Austin A50 Cambridges and many 1960s BMC models. By the end of the 1970s, however, a reshuffle/rationalization within Pressed Steel Fisher resulted in the stamping and assembly of Jaguar body shells being moved from Cowley and Swindon to the Castle Bromwich site.

By the time that Jaguar was privatized in 1984, the Castle Bromwich workforce was concerned only with the assembly and painting of Jaguar monocoques – these being the XJ6/XJ12 saloons, and the sporty XJ-S units. By no means all of the site was fully occupied (this made the short-lived setting up of Jaguar's pressings venture with GKN, at Telford, rather difficult to understand), which explains why Ford, which had owned Jaguar from 1989, was so ready to clear some of it, and to build a brand-new assembly block for the next generation of Jaguars in the late 1990s. By 2008, a much expanded Castle Bromwich plant was also building XF and XJ saloons.

From the very beginning, the XK8 monocoques were always pressed and assembled at Castle Bromwich before being transported to Browns Lane for painting, trimming and final assembly. The same buildings also supplied modified platforms to Motor Panels Ltd of Coventry so that Aston Martin DB7 coupé and Volante shells could take shape.

feature of the finalized car – the 'sail panels', or 'flying buttresses' linking the top corners of the roof to the tail lamps, along the top of the rear wings – was apparently inspired by what Jaguar's much respected aerodynamicist Malcolm Sayer had recommended to ensure straight-line stability in high-speed running.

Other features were all developments of current European trends – these including the use of a sharply cut-off tail (related, no question, to that of the XJ6 saloon), and of rhomboidal headlamps or (in the case of USA-market cars) pairs of smaller, circular headlamps – and by the time every aspect was approved by Jaguar, and then by the main British Leyland board, 1972 was well advanced. The shape and equipment of the interior followed on, but all was decided upon by 1973.

Even though Jaguar was badly shaken by the financial traumas that struck British Leyland in 1974/1975 – the colossus ran out of money (mainly because the mass-production side, otherwise known as Austin-Morris, was in a shambolic, not to say anarchic, state), had to dash to the British government for support, and was finally taken into public ownership in the spring of 1975 – development of the XJ27/XJ-S project went ahead without delay, and the new car was launched in September 1975.

At that time, the original XJ-S was available only with a fuel-injected 285bhp version of the 5.3-litre V12 engine (this figure was reduced to 244bhp when the car was sold in North America, because of all the exhaust emission limitations of that market place), and with a choice of four-speed manual gearbox (from the E-Type) or a three-speed Borg Warner automatic transmission.

It was interesting to note that in this car, demand for the manual transmission was always very limited. At this point, too, it is worth recalling that even on the last of the E-Types there had been an increasing tendency to order automatic transmission types, too! Certainly one reason was that the existing Jaguar 'stick-shift' gearbox was none too

refined; however, the main reason was that the market place was swinging strongly in favour of automatic transmission cars, particularly in North America where the majority of sales were being made.

XJ-S – an Eventful Career

Deliveries of the XJ-S to European customers began almost at once, but the first cars did not reach the USA until early 1976. Although the XJ-S might always have had a controversial career, and its public image went through several peaks and troughs, it would then remain in production for nearly twenty-one years, and no fewer than 115,330 cars of all types would eventually be delivered. I think it is important that I now trace the most important junctions in that long life, as many of them had an effect on replacement cars (which included the XK8) that followed. Sections in *italics* indicate those parts of the XJ-S story that would have a significant bearing on the XK8.

In the face of tiny, and steadily declining sales, the manual transmission option was finally withdrawn in March 1979:

Power train chief Harry Mundy had finally lost his long battle to get approval for an all-new five-speed manual transmission that he had designed, and of which several prototypes were already installed in test cars. This was the first step, at Jaguar, towards buying in proprietary manual transmissions for its cars. First of all, the Rover SD1 gearbox (which was not strong enough to withstand V12 engine torque) was adopted for XJ6 saloon models. Then from 1983, when the AJ6-engined XJ-SC Cabriolet cars came along, a Getrag five-speed transmission would become available.

There was no shame in doing this – BMW, for instance, was already doing the same, and the Getrag company basked in attracting business from both concerns.

In the meantime, and in reaction to the influence of the second energy crisis of 1979 (when, to coin a suitable USA-originated phrase, 'the Shah left town' and an Iranian political revolution ensued…), Jaguar pushed ahead with work on making the V12 more economical. This led to the launch of the XJ-S HE (high efficiency) model, which appeared in July 1981.

This was not before time, as demand for the XJ-S had plunged to a new low in 1980, when only 1,057 cars had been produced: for a time, in fact, production ceased altogether, and there was a distinct possibility that the model might even have been abandoned, after a career of only five years.

With innovation, and an increased attention to fuel economy in mind, this was the period in which first thoughts were given to a replacement for the XJ-S models. Styling of a brace of new models, coded XJ41 and XJ42, began in 1980, these being the new sporty Jaguars that would occupy much time, development, and investment capital throughout the 1980s. The style of these cars, which was initially approved by British Leyland's main Board, was signed off in July 1982. The evolution of their looks would eventually be a very strong influence on the Aston Martin DB7 and the XK8 that followed in the 1990s.

The turn-around then began, slowly, steadily and eventually with great vigour, because in the next ten years demand, and production, would soar, such that more than 11,000 cars were to be built in the peak year of 1989.

One important factor was that two major innovations were brought forward in 1983. One was to introduce the first of several different types of soft-top XJ-S types – this being the XJ-SC Cabriolet – and the other was for Jaguar to launch their all-new 6-cylinder engine, the AJ6 type. This engine, incidentally, would not be made available in US-market XJ-S/XJS types until 1992.

The decision to choose a Cabriolet, rather than a full convertible style, was taken after considering what torsional rigidity would remain after the hacksaws had come out. Without spending a fair fortune in time, development and investment capital in altering the body shell, Jaguar's engineers were originally not convinced that they could ever produce an acceptable drop-top model. Rather than go for a full convertible style at this stage, therefore, Jaguar elected to produce the XJ-S Cabriolet instead, where there would still be a substantial welded framework surrounding the passenger cabin. It would be possible for top and rear panels to be removed, but side windows would be retained, and there was effectively a sturdy roll-bar above and behind the front seats. Some extra reinforcement was added under the floor pan, but not as much as would have been needed with a full convertible conversion.

By the early 1990s, the XJ-S had not only been on sale for more than fifteen years, but had been considerably retouched around the rear quarters. Over in North America, it continued to sell well until 1996.

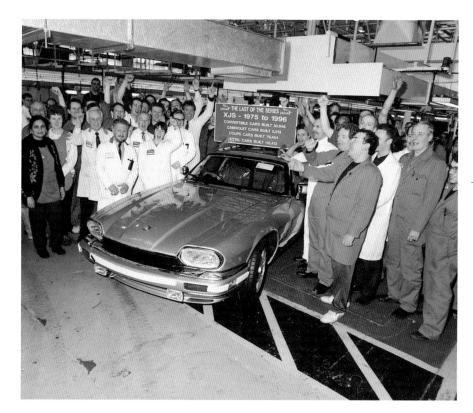

Jaguar ceremonially brought the XJS's career to a close in April 1996, when the final two cars – a silver-blue coupé and…

…a red convertible dropped off the assembly line at Browns Lane on the same day. The caption tells us that no fewer than 115,413 XJSs of all types had been produced – but later there was a recount, which revised that figure to 115,330.

On the same day as the last XJSs were produced (though this picture was not released to the media) Jaguar also posed a dark green pilot-production XK8 between the XJSs.

This was the first time that a Jaguar XJ-S had been produced without the distinctive 'flying buttresses' at the rear quarter of the bodyshell. In spite of Malcolm Sayer's earlier prognostications about the stability features that the buttresses conferred to an XJ-S, there do not seem to have been any complaints about the stability of the Cabriolet derivative. If Malcolm Sayer had not insisted that they be fitted on the original cars, they might never have been considered, and once removed, the need for such add-ons was soon discounted.

XK Sports Cars

When the XK180 project car was launched in 1998, Jaguar was happy to recall the heritage of the line of two-seater 'XK…' sports cars that had started it all immediately after World War II. Indeed, one of the reasons given for choosing this name was that it would recall the launch of the original XK120, which had appeared almost exactly fifty years earlier.

The XK120 of 1948 was the first-ever Jaguar sports car to be powered by what became the legendary twin-overhead-camshaft 6-cylinder XK engine, a 3.4-litre unit for which 160bhp was claimed. Like all other Jaguars of the day, it was personally shaped by William Lyons himself, and even before deliveries began, a top speed of more than 120mph (190km/h) was publicly demonstrated.

In 1954 the XK140 took over from the XK120, and was closely based on it, with almost identical styling. Although it was always obvious that one type was an evolution of the other, the XK140 had more power, more creature comforts and more interior passenger space, and there were more derivatives.

The XK150 of 1957 was the third major derivative of this illustrious breed, retaining the same 102in wheelbase chassis and XK-engine installation, though with a somewhat changed exterior body style. Before the last XK150 of all was built in 1961, some versions had engines that had been enlarged to 3.8 litres, with triple SU carburettors, and a claimed 265bhp. The top speed of these cars was now more than 135mph (210km/h).

There was no XK130, of course, and although one or two references were made (outside the factory, it must be admitted) to an 'XK160' being developed, the next Jaguar sports car to appear would be the sensational new E-Type.

This aerial view of Browns Lane, Allesley (taken from the north-east of the plant), shows the way that Jaguar had persistently enlarged the plant since taking over in 1951. The original 'ex-Daimler' factory may be identified by its black roof, with all the remainder being later additions. The historic administrative block, including the chairman's office, is in the centre right of the shot.

Although the new AJ6 6-cylinder engine would never figure in the XK8 range, it was nevertheless important to the still-developing story of the XJ-S, and the cars that would, one day, inspire the birth of the XK8. It was only the third all-new Jaguar road car engine of all time, for the XK power unit of 1948 had been the first, and the V12 power unit of 1971 had been the second. Crucially, it would also be used as the engine around which the stillborn XJ41/XJ42 models were engineered, and it would also be the first engine to be used in the XJ-S-based Aston Martin DB7 model (*see* the Appendix).

The development of the AJ6 6-cylinder engine took ages to come to fruition. Originally conceived in 1970 (when Walter Hassan and Harry Mundy were leading personalities in the engine design area), and effectively one bank of the new V12 engine, it did not take on a separate life of its own until 1976, by which time most direct links with the V12 had been lost. From this point there were to be 12-valve single-overhead-camshaft types, and a 24-valve twin-cam type, both of them on similar light-alloy cylinder blocks, in 2.9-litre, 3.6-litre and eventually 4-litre sizes. First seen in the XJ-SC of 1983, it was then adopted for the 'new generation XJ40' generation of saloons in 1986. After a comprehensive redesign it then became AJ16 in 1994, one version was supercharged for use in the Aston Martin DB7 launched in the same year, and it was finally used in the DB7 of 1999/2000.

In the meantime, over in the USA the demand for fully convertible bodies had doubled, and redoubled, so much so that a North American coachwork specialist, Hess & Eisenhardt, was encouraged by Jaguar-USA to launch a full convertible version of the XJ-S (which it manufactured by cutting, carving and stiffening already built coupés), this type being launched in 1986. Such cars were in production for two years, and no fewer than 2,000 such hybrids were manufactured: they were all sold in North America, and never seen in Europe.

For many years, Jaguar had merely been a subsidiary of a larger industrial group – BMH since 1966, and British Leyland from 1968 – so it seemed that the company could never take new model and major investment decisions without having to refer them to the parent Board of Directors. It must have come as a delightful surprise, then, when the British government, which still controlled British Leyland at the time, decided to cut off Jaguar from the rest of the group, to privatize it, and to let it find its own destiny.

That much anticipated day came in May 1984, and it was amazing to see just how the atmosphere, and the enthusiasm, lifted so quickly in the business. In the meantime, the launch of the XJ41/XJ42 cars was linked to that of the new generation saloons, and would initially be timed for two years afterwards – if the saloon's launch date was delayed, that of the new sporting Jaguars was sure to suffer.

One of Jaguar's earliest post-privatization decisions was then to get the new generation XJ40-type saloon on to the market, after which it turned its attention to the XJ-S again. To replace not only the American Hess & Eisenhardt conversion, but the XJ-SC Cabriolet as well, a fully convertible XJ-S was finally brought to market in March 1988. Much of the work on the re-engineering of the body shell to produce a stiff and satisfactory soft top had been carried out by Karmann of Germany. In the end, Jaguar admitted that one third of the body panels were either new, or very substantially modified, which explains why they had always shied away from tackling this project before then.

All doubts about the wisdom of reintroducing a full convertible alternative to the coupé style had finally been swept away. This meant that when the time came, there would always be coupé and convertible version of XJ41 and XJ42, and when those cars, too, were abandoned, there would always be convertible and coupé versions of the final XK8.

Once of Jaguar's biggest rivals for sales in the USA, Mercedes-Benz, must have smiled quietly at

By the late 1980s, the XJ-S had already been on sale for more than ten years, but it was still a sleek and impressive car. When the time came to engineer the XK8, it was decided to use the self-same platform for the new model.

all these goings-on, for in the 1980s they had taken a converse decision. This was the time when they actually dropped a hard-top coupé version of their 450SL (the 450SLC) in favour of continuing to build the convertible type alone. That car, which had an equally long career, would still be going strong when replaced at the end of the 1980s.

In the meantime, Jaguar was so delighted with the work done for them by Karmann that when the time came to commission a new phase of XJ41/XJ42 cars, Karmann was chosen to build the body shells for those cars (see Chapter 2).

Unhappily, Jaguar was already finding it difficult to carry on developing new models as a privatized business, not because the business was unprofitable – on the contrary, and in the short term, the company was making good money – but it was rapidly becoming clear that it simply could not afford to invest in the new models it needed, of which XJ41/XJ42 was one family.

Jaguar's chairman, Sir John Egan, made little secret of his search for a partner during 1989, and during the summer/autumn something of

As slightly restyled in the early 1990s, the XJS had a more rounded rump and a different side-window profile, although the basic dimensions, and the cabin itself, were not significantly altered.

a bidding war for control developed between two American giants – Ford and General Motors. Quite characteristically for that period, GM dithered over an offer price, and how much control it actually needed. Ford, on the other handed, offered no less than £1.6 billion in a 'knock-out' bid which caused GM to withdraw from the fight, and for Jaguar to accept the offer with some alacrity. The take-over/rescue was finalized in November 1989, and Ford immediately started a root-and-branch review of the company it had just bought.

Within months Ford had homed in on the XJ41/XJ42 projects, decided that these cars had become too large and bulky, too heavy, and – by definition – likely to be too expensive, so the project was finally, and irrevocably, cancelled. The search for an eventual successor to the XJ-S models, which had now been going on for a full decade, had failed. It was at this point, therefore, that thoughts began of the car that would become the XK8.

Ford, on the other hand, was not about to kill off the brand it had so expensively bought, so instead of pushing ahead with XJ41/XJ42, it authorized immediate priority of work on a heavily revised and 'tail-lifted' (as opposed to 'facelifted', for most of the change was found at the rear of the car instead!) XJ-S. Design and engineering work that had already been

In the early 1980s, TWR's XJ-S race cars built up a formidable reputation in European Touring car racing.

XJS types joining the final assembly tracks at Browns Lane – the XK8 would be built up on the same tracks.

completed was speedily approved, and the much revised XJS (note that the XJ-S title had contracted into XJS at this time) was introduced in April 1991.

Because the platform, the choice of engines and the running gear was all to be carried forward (the 3.6-litre engine was enlarged to 4-litre at that point, however), most of the changes were confined to the body style and its engineering. Although the Coupé's ever-controversial flying buttresses were retained, there was a new shape and profile to the side windows, while at the rear there were new and rather more smoothly detailed shapes to the rear quarters, this including new-shape tail lamps and rear wings to match.

At this time it was interesting to learn that Jaguar and Ford had indeed considered abandoning the buttresses. Jaguar stylist Colin Holtum once told the author that coupés without buttresses had indeed been built, and shown to a selection of typical Jaguar owners in carefully controlled 'clinic' conditions, but that: 'The public told us they preferred the coupé to have its buttresses, so we retained them on the latest car. Without them – well, it just didn't look like an XJ-S, somehow.'

Once it was launched, Jaguar somehow kept the XJS well to the fore, especially in the USA, and for a time all suggestions that it would eventually be replaced were firmly ignored. Yet Jaguar knew that it would have to do something,

and soon, for the hard-used production tooling was now approaching its twentieth birthday, and needed more and more preventative
maintenance to keep it working well. The V12
engine, in particular, was already living on borrowed time, for it was not able to pass the proposed exhaust emission rules that were due to
come into force in the USA in 1995. A tentative proposal to give the existing car one final
tweak by making it the first car to use the all-
new AJ-V8 engine, which was in its final
stages, was soon abandoned.

*With all work on the XJ41 and XJ42 projects
firmly abandoned, and work on the revision of the
XJ6 saloons now paramount, Jaguar's development
team had no time to spend on a new sports car project. Until, that is, Project X100 took shape, first of all
on paper only, then as a styling study, and ultimately
as an active project. Such projects rarely leap out as a
ready-to-go programme, but project director Bob Dover
later put the 'lift-off' point at April/May 1996.*

The XJS, meantime, had entered its final
'long goodbye' phase. In the beginning the
face-lifted car had been available with a choice
of 223bhp/4-litre straight-six, or 290bhp/5.3-
litre V12 engines, and with full convertible or
coupé body styles, though the 4-litre Convertible did not become available until May
1992. A 6-cylinder-engined XJS finally went
on sale in the USA in the winter of 1992/1993
(that was almost ten years after the AJ6 engine
had originally been seen on domestic and
European-market cars).

The long-lived V12 engine then received its
final makeover in May 1993, when it became
a 308bhp/6-litre type; and finally, in June
1994, Jaguar converted the 6-cylinder engines
from AJ6 to AJ16 which, in 4-litre form, meant
that the XJS now had 241bhp. V12 engine
manufacture ceased in 1995 (just as the 1991
forecast had stated that it would have to do so),
and the very last XJS types of all were built at
Browns Lane in April 1996.

Total XJS production, from 1975 to 1996
inclusive, had been 115,330, and Jaguar had
every intention of making and selling more of
the new type XK8s than that.

2 False Start – XJ41 and XJ42

If the cars we still know as the XJ41 and XJ42 (they were never officially badged throughout their lives) had made it into the showrooms, then the XK8 might never have appeared. On the other hand, if XJ41 and XJ42 had never been designed and partly developed, the shape of the XK8 might have been very different – and the Aston Martin DB7 might never have existed at all. Yet the two ranges were very different, not only in their looks, but also in their engineering and their marketing stance.

So, let us take a deep breath, and wind back our mental clocks to the 1980s, which opened when Jaguar was still a subsidiary of the loss-making British Leyland conglomerate, when its reputation for product quality had plumbed the depths, and because of that, when the company's very survival was already being questioned.

To remind you all: in 1980 the XJ-S had been in production for five years, and John (later Sir John) Egan had just joined the company with a stark and simple mission: to save it from extinction – this at a time when the XJ-S was selling so slowly that only 1,057 cars would be built in the whole of that year.

As already related, this was the period in which Jaguar's marketing team was still smarting at the wave of criticism they had received from the pundits, for replacing the gorgeous E-Type with the larger XJ-S, by replacing the so-called aerodynamically styled E-Type by the more craggily shaped XJ-S. In the short term, however, nothing could be done to replace the XJ-S – the financial realities of product cycles, more important new-car projects, a lack of investment capital, and even

This was the way that Jaguar's stylists were thinking in the late 1980s, and the themes would certainly read across to the XJ41/XJ42 shape at the same time. This was the prototype XJ220 of 1988.

Jaguar's curvaceous style changed gradually, but persistently, between the 1950s and the late 1980s – from front to rear this was the C-Type race car, the D-Type race car, the stillborn XJ13 race car, and the XJ220.

wounded pride, had a lot to do with this – but there was a growing conviction that something better, more shapely and more visually exciting might eventually be developed.

Not only that, but at the time there was a growing conviction within the company that the controversial XJ-S was too large and too heavy. Any new model, it was reasoned, should go back some way towards the character of the much-loved E-Type – it should be lighter, smaller, and more sinuously beautiful. Even so, it was not until mid-1980 that any proposals – merely paper proposals, I should emphasize – for such a car were ever circulated.

In so many ways, as we now know, 1980 was, in fact, a pivotal year for Jaguar. First of all, John Egan was getting to grips with the quality problems, especially from some of his more

When the XJ41/XJ42 cars were being developed in the 1980s, it was always intended that they should use one or other versions of the modern 6-cylinder AJ6 engine – here seen, in supercharged form, in the XJR saloon of the 1990s.

complacent suppliers ('I actually managed to convince wheel suppliers that their wheels should be round'), so that slowly (but very slowly) sales and customer confidence began to build up again. The year 1980 was a low point in so many ways – but then there was a massive recovery in the 1980s.

Of equal importance was the fact that at this time the design staff, and Jaguar management, had finally got the new-generation saloon (we knew it, then, as the XJ40 project) to the point where its style was signed off, the engineering developments were in place and where – provisionally at least – they thought it could be brought to market in 1984, though this date would slip back to 1986 before the car was finally launched.

To all the forward-thinkers – the visionaries, if you will – this therefore opened a window where the future of Jaguar's most sporting machines – coupés and convertibles – could be reconsidered. Perhaps it was too much to hope that approval for a true 'F-Type' two-seater could ever be forced through the upper hierarchy of British Leyland, but the attempt could surely be made? It was at this point that two project codes – XJ41 and XJ42 – began to circulate.

Even so, by the summer of 1980 stylist Keith Helfet (we will hear that name many times during the unfolding of the XK8 story) had produced the first visual studies of what a new 'XJ41' sports car might look like – the truly crucial assumption being that the body shell could be based on a shortened version of the platform/underbody of the forthcoming 'XJ40', which was totally different from that of the existing XJ-S. A paragraph in the *XJ40 Programme Submission* dated 2 February 1981 and circulated within Jaguar, had this to say: 'XJ40 componentry and under-frame can be readily adapted to provide, at minimum cost and within a relatively short time period, additional model ranges, namely a luxury performance sports car and a smaller executive saloon.'

Because of a serious shortage of investment capital at Jaguar, however, little came of this at the time. It was not until mid-1982 that,

initially only on paper, and in full-scale clay models, that two parallel new cars – we would come to know them as XJ41 (a fastback coupé – the hatchback feature would be added later) and XJ42 (a convertible derivative) – began to evolve.

The theme – inasmuch as a theme yet existed in any concrete form – was that there should be two different body-shell variants: a two-door convertible and a 2+2 Targa-type. The convertible would be a pure two-seater with a fold-down soft top, which would leave the cockpit fully opened when lowered. The Targa would have a detachable roof section but solid pressed-steel quarters and roll-over bars (like the Porsche 911 Targa – hence the choice of name), where the detachable panel could be stowed in the boot, rather than left back at home in the garage.

Radford – Jaguar's Engines Powerhouse

In Coventry, almost everyone connected with the motor industry knew Jaguar's Radford plant as 'The Daimler', for this is where Daimler private cars, military vehicles and buses had been built for many years. Daimler's automotive business had been absorbed by BSA in 1910, and a new factory in the Radford district of Coventry was set up in 1912. The business expanded strongly in the next fifty years, and was centred on Radford, though bodies came from elsewhere.

Jaguar needed more factory space in 1960, and BSA was ready to divest itself of Daimler, so the deal was done. In the next few years, Daimler private car assembly was concentrated on Jaguar's earlier site at Browns Lane, while Radford was redeveloped as the centre of Jaguar engine and transmission manufacture, assembly and testing.

When Ford took over Jaguar at the end of 1989, Radford's main products were the V12 and AJ6 6-cylinder engines. V12 assembly ended in 1997, AJ6/AJ16 assembly followed at the same time, and although Jaguar themselves wanted to install the new AJ-V8 facility there, Ford had other ideas and sold off the entire site. The factory buildings no longer exist.

It was always intended that the new cars should be lighter, lower, sleeker and visually smaller (if not all that much smaller) than the XJ-S, and that they should look more like visual descendants of the much loved E-Type. Although Jaguar's aerodynamicist Malcolm Sayer could not be involved (he had died, much missed, in 1970), and his mathematical treatment of styling lines and shapes could therefore not be employed, it was always hoped that the new cars could follow a similar philosophy of bulks and proportions.

Because of the prevailing atmosphere within the industry regarding drag coefficients – the soaring cost of vehicle fuels had made a big impression – XJ41 was meant to be much more wind-cheating than its predecessors. In spite of its so-called 'aerodynamic' shaping, incidentally, the E-Type had always been disappointing and had always been a high-drag car, the XJ-S had a coefficient of about 0.38, and it was hoped to get XJ41 down towards the 0.30 mark (which Audi was then repeatedly trumpeting for its new-generation 100 saloon). High hopes, maybe, because that figure would never be approached.

One obvious and lasting influence on the shape of the cars that were to evolve was the Pininfarina Jaguar XJ-S Spider, which had been unveiled at the Birmingham Motor Show, way back in October 1978. Although Jaguar had no immediate intention of putting such a car into production (nor did they have the funds to make it so!), with their tacit approval, an XJ-S had been supplied to Turin, on which Pininfarina was given a free rein to work its magic. That car, which ran on a lightly modified XJ-S platform (the petrol tank had been moved, but almost all the rest of the 'chassis' was left as standard) was an astonishingly sleek two-seater.

As my old colleagues on *Autocar* wrote about this car at the time:

> The bodywork is very obviously smooth and free from protruberances into the air-stream. The pronounced tips smoothing airflow front and back of

the wheels are also carried over [from the 'aerodynamic' prototype of the 1970s], as are the upswept sides between the wheels.... The Pininfarina body is all steel and is designed to have flexible plastic front and rear end sections, à la Porsche 928, in place of conventional bumpers. Pininfarina make special mention of the oval front air intake as a reminder of Jaguar traditions.

First Thoughts

Whereas the XJ-S had been based closely on the existing platform architecture and running gear of the Jaguar XJ6/XJ12 saloons of the 1970s, the layout of the XJ41 and XJ42 was meant to look ahead, rather than backwards into tradition. Right from the start, it was always assumed that these cars would be based on a shortened version of the still-under-development XJ40 saloon, which would take over in the mid-1980s. Although the basic layout of the new cars was to be derived from that of the old XJ-S – in particular in the layout of front and rear suspensions – the 6-cylinder engine, the choice of transmissions and many technical details would all be modified versions of the XJ40 type.

At that point, therefore, XJ41 would have used the brand new 6-cylinder AJ6 3.6-litre engine, still in normally aspirated guise, which would be backed by familiar Getrag manual or ZF automatic transmissions, all built up around XJ40 platform pressings, front and rear suspension and steering. Incidentally, and since this project was initiated immediately after the second Middle East 'oil shock'/energy crisis had hit the world's motor industry, at that point the use of Jaguar's impressive, but thirsty, existing V12 engine was never even considered.

In the beginning, of course, it was styling, rather than engineering, that gained priority, with the months – the seasons, even – passing with no sign of the first running prototype. All such design work was carried out in house, at Browns Lane, with Keith Helfet as the senior designer behind the team – though of course the evolution of this project would eventually drag on for so long that it would all be transferred to the dedicated Whitley engineering centre, elsewhere in Coventry, which Jaguar eventually occupied from the late 1980s.

There is no doubt that the shape of the XJ41/XJ42 was strongly influenced by the Pininfarina car, and by 1982 the lines were beginning to settle down. It is important to note, by the way, that even though Jaguar's founder, Sir William Lyons, had now been retired for more than ten years, Jaguar happily received him on regular visits to the factory styling studios, and that full size mock-ups were

Jim Randle was Jaguar's much respected director of engineering in the 1980–1990 period. Much admired for the work his team did in finalizing the new-generation XJ6 (the XJ40 project) at the time, they were criticized for allowing the weight of the XJ41/XJ42 cars to run away during their development phase.

This was the final shape of the XJ41 Coupé project of the late 1980s. The resemblance to the later XK8 is clear, though there were no shared panels.

The XJ42 project of the late 1980s was a sleek convertible, which would eventually donate some of its styling 'cues' to the XK8 Convertible that followed.

The XJ41/XJ42 project used a turbocharged version of the AJ6 6-cylinder engine. Although this was certainly considered for the forthcoming XK8, it was rejected in favour of an all-new V8 engine.

sometimes taken out to his home, at Wappenbury Hall, not far from Leamington Spa, where they could be viewed, in privacy, away from public gaze, but against real buildings, with real countryside in the background.

Although detail changes continued to be made to the style, the new type always looked (and was) totally different from the existing XJ-S, not only in the general lines of the new shells, but with the use of headlamps set well back in the front wings, rather as they had originally been in the E-Type (there were proposals, too, that they might have been placed behind swivel/pop-up covers), and with moulded front panels – whereas the XJ-S had exposed headlamps, a bluff front end and separate chrome bumpers.

Dimensions changed little at this point, including a wheelbase of 102in (2,591mm), an overall length of 181.4in (4,608mm), and a width of 70.9in (1,800mm) (no 'over-mirror' dimensions were included at that point in history), and all would be retained, except in minor detail, when the XK8 eventually came along. The one failing, caused by the way the sleek rear end was styled, was that the available boot space was small, at 8cu ft (0.23cu m) – much less than the 10.6cu ft (0.3cu m) of the existing XJ-S.

Although XJ41, in other words, was always much the same size as the XJ-S – it cast a similar 'shadow', so to speak – the new cars were meant to be considerably lighter than their ancestor, this being emphasized by the choice of the new 3.6-litre AJ6 6-cylinder engine. In

1982 (and, to be honest, before a running prototype was constructed), Jaguar forecast that the new car might weigh no more than 3,280lb/1,488kg.

Design and styling of the two distinctly different types − the Targa/fastback coupé, and the full convertible − went ahead at the same time, for Jaguar was quite determined to bring back open-top motoring to their range. It is worth recalling that there was an open top and a coupé version of the original E-Type, and that the coupé was dropped in 1973/1974, leaving an open two-seater to bring the E-Type's career to an end in 1975. On the other hand, when the Jaguar XJ-S was put on sale, it was only originally sold as a hard-top coupé − and the half-and-half Cabriolet did not appear until 1983, neither would the full factory Convertible go on sale until 1988.

By the mid-1980s, however, there had been so many delays that this project was really very little nearer to fruition than it had been in 1980. Keith Helfet, as patient and pragmatic as all such senior designers/stylists have to be, continued to retouch the car from time to time, but after four years had seen no more than 'see-through' glass-fibre mock-ups built.

Jaguar was privatized in 1984 − and thankfully lost all links with the remainder of the British Leyland concern − when a new programme was approved, with a view to pilot production getting under way in May 1988, and a launch in the UK forecast towards the end of 1988. Because the planners had now concluded that more power was required, a twin-turbocharged version of the 4-litre engine (it would be rated at 330bhp at 5,000rpm) was added to the profile of the new models. A new department − New Vehicle Concepts (NVC) − was set up in 1985, and took responsibility for the XJ41's progress.

Because little money had so far been expended on this project (it was Jaguar's much-respected engineering chief William Heynes, no less, who once said that: 'Paper is cheap, but cutting metal is expensive'), NVC effectively started again, beefing up the entire concept. Sending the style back to Jaguar's design studios, they urged Helfet to widen the scope of the theme, not only to allow more cooling air to be encouraged into and through the engine bay, and to provide more cabin space, but even more significantly, they decided to develop a four-wheel-drive system to transmit all the power. Costs, complications and vehicle weight all increased inexorably − and it wasn't long before the team decided to abandon the idea of using a modified XJ40 platform in favour of specialized engineering.

But, four-wheel drive? Why so? At this time Porsche and Mercedes-Benz, after all, were managing to sell many more such high-performance cars than Jaguar, and did not need four-wheel drive. Neither then, nor later, did Jaguar come up with a convincing reason for this decision, which is a pity, because this was a major failing as far as the next owners, Ford, were concerned.

Renowned development engineer Peter Taylor, then working at Jaguar, later had this to say: 'The first thing that [NVC] asked their computers was about four-wheel drive. "If you really want to make a car with 350bhp, you'd better make it four-wheel drive or its tyres will be on fire before the lights go green." Clever as they were, these computers had never driven a car.'

It is worth noting that at this point Jaguar had little or no four-wheel-drive expertise of their own (before 1984 they could, presumably, have consulted Land-Rover, for both companies were still part of the BL Group), but there was, at least, much independent expertise available in Coventry. FF Developments (originally Harry Ferguson Research) were heavily embroiled in such work for Ford on Sierra XR4×4 and RS200 models, and had also been consulted when the MG Metro 6R4 rally car was being developed.

First Prototypes

Finally, in 1988, Jaguar commissioned the building of three working prototypes of body shells − they were coded as CC1, CC2 and CC3 (the

'CC' stood for 'Concept Car') – from the independent company Karmann, of West Germany. These body shells would finally be delivered back to Browns Lane in 1989 – and it is worth noting that nine years had already passed between the 'Why don't we…?' meetings, and the acceptance of the first cars that actually ran.

Some things, however, could be done much faster at Jaguar. It was in the same period, from the mid-1980s, that the mid-engined XJ220 had been conceived, built, put on show at the first NEC Motor Show, then farmed out to Tom Walkinshaw's JaguarSport. The proposed production car was unveiled at the end of 1989.

One of these prototypes eventually went to the high-speed Nardo proving grounds in the south of Italy, where CC1, with the twin-

This was the last, and therefore the definitive, style of the XJ41 project. Although there were distinct resemblances to the XK8 that would follow, notable differences included the covered-up headlamps, the headlamp shapes themselves, and the two-piece, rather than single-piece, front grille.

Jaguar XJ41/XJ42 (Late Prototype, *circa* 1989)

Layout	Unit-construction steel body/chassis structure. 2+2-seater, front engine/rear drive, to be sold as a two-door closed coupé or convertible	*Suspension and steering*	
		Front	Independent coil springs, wishbones, anti-roll bar, telescopic dampers
		Rear	Independent double coil springs, fixed-length drive shafts, lower wishbones, radius arms, anti-roll bar, twin telescopic dampers
Engine			
Type	Jaguar AJ16 family, much modified	Steering	Rack and pinion, power-assisted
Block material	Cast aluminium	Wheels	Cast aluminium disc, bolt-on
Head material	Cast aluminium	Rim width	8in
Cylinders	6, in-line arrangement		
Cooling	Water	*Brakes*	
Bore and stroke	91 × 102mm	Type	Disc brakes at front and rear (ventilated at front), with vacuum servo assistance and anti-lock
Capacity	3980cc		
Main bearings	7		
Valves	4 per cylinder, operated by twin-overhead-camshafts per cylinder head, with hydraulic phasing of cam timing, and inverted bucket-type tappets		
		Dimensions (in/mm)	
Compression ratio	8.5:1	Wheelbase	102.0/2,591
Fuel supply	Zytec fuel injection/engine management system, with twin turbochargers and intercooler	Overall length	181.0/4,597
		Overall width	73.0/1,854
		Overall height	48.0/1,219
Max. power	330bhp (DIN) @ 5,000rpm	Unladen weight	
Max. torque	380lb/ft @ 3,000rpm	(coupé)	4,063lb/1,847kg
Transmission	Choice of Getrag five-speed manual transmission, or four-speed ZF automatic transmission (four-wheel drive, considered until 1989, had been abandoned)	*Estimated performance*	
		Maximum speed	160mph/258km/h
		0–60mph	5.9sec

---

turbocharged 4-litre engine, recorded 175mph (265km/h) and seemed to be totally unstressed at the end of the tests. This, of itself, was encouraging, but somehow the impetus had already gone from the programme.

By this time (mid-1989) the four-wheel-drive installation had already been abandoned, and it was becoming clear that the project, as it stood, was not only spiralling out of management control, but out of favour. By this time the hatchback coupé weighed 4,063lb/1,847kg, which was nearly 300lb/136kg heavier than the 4-litre XJS was to be – not much lighter, as had originally been intended.

At almost exactly the same time that Ford took control of Jaguar – in November 1989 – NVC formally handed over the XJ41/XJ42 project to Jaguar's mainstream engineers who, not to exaggerate their reaction, were appalled by what they discovered. Not only were they unhappy with the way the cars had put on so much weight in the 1980s, they were also disturbed by the less-than-perfect packaging, and a lack of interior space and

Ford – the Saviour

For the first few years after privatization in 1984, Jaguar's future looked to be set fair. By 1989, though, all the financial indicators were pointing the wrong way, Jaguar was profitable though under-capitalized, and chairman Sir John Egan was happy to look around for a partner.

Two North American giants, Ford and General Motors, both fought for control, the contest eventually being won because Ford was decisive while GM dithered. Some financial observers suggest that Ford paid far too much for Jaguar, but the fact is that that price included the immeasurable goodwill of a truly charismatic name.

Fortunately for Jaguar enthusiasts, Ford never committed any of the sins that the doom-mongers suggested would follow. There was no instant 'badge-engineering', and no dilution of the 'Jaguar-ness' of the cars. As the 1990s developed, Ford not only paid all the bills and stemmed the losses, but financed the development of the much-changed 1991-variety XJS, followed it up with approval for the latest generation XJ6 range of saloons, then committed huge amounts of capital investment for the new generation V8 engine and the XK8 range to be put on sale.

Unhappily for all Jaguar enthusiasts, Ford found it difficult to turn Jaguar into a much larger and more profitable business, so soon after the XK8 was discontinued, Ford let it be known that they were ready to sell the brand to another 'sugar daddy'. Even though Jaguar had become increasingly close to Land Rover (the two companies eventually shared engines and design/development facilities), Ford decided to dispose of JLR, completing the disposal to the Tata Group of India in March 2008.

overall visibility from the driving seat. Things did not look promising.

By March 1990 it was all over. Even before Ford's top management moved in to Browns Lane to carry out a complete review of the company they had just purchased, Jaguar itself was already looking unfavourably at the XJ41/XJ42 project. The fact was that, after nearly ten years, the new car still lacked a lot of detail development, still lacked influential backers – and was still faced by an ageing, but still graceful, XJ-S project, which continued to be a success.

Faced with much evidence, much of it unfavourable, Ford agreed that the XJ41/XJ42 project should be scrapped, and that a complete late-life revision of the XJ-S (which became XJS, with significant restyling and re-engineering) should go ahead instead, at full speed. The story of that car has already been told, but the story of what became the XK8 was only just about to begin.

3 Engineering the XK8

After the XJ41/XJ42 project was cancelled, Jaguar's stylists, engineers and planners drew back a little, licked their wounds, saw that the XJS was still manfully holding on to first place as far as sales were concerned – and waited for a chance to try again. But this did not – could not – happen for a time, for in this period Jaguar's efforts went into revisions to the saloon car range. Although this new car – X300 in 'Jaguar-speak', and effectively a full-on redesign of the existing XJ6/XJ12 saloon range – had cost Jaguar £300 million to prepare, had involved the refinement or modification of many different skin panels and saw the return of

Jaguar's easily recognized four-headlamp nose, it was developed without reference to anything that the sports car engineers might have had in mind.

What it *did* do, however, was to take up most of the engineering staff's time at Whitley. In styling, in engineering, in development and – equally important in these times – in legislative detail, there was little slack in any department. It was not until 1991/1992 that Jaguar at Whitley, now steered by Jim Padilla and Clive Ennos (both ex-Ford, ex-USA and ex-Europe respectively), could try again. This time around, however, there would be a new

---

The Whitley Technical Centre

Like many other industrial buildings in Coventry, the Whitley facility was originally built with military aircraft production in mind, and the area was used as a grass airfield from 1918. When it was first built, to the south-east of Coventry's city centre, it was well clear of any housing and was used for aircraft testing in the 1920s, and later – after the first major buildings were erected – for aircraft component manufacture by the Armstrong-Whitworth business. By the end of the 1930s, Coventry suburbia had arrived on its boundaries, and was only kept at bay by the building of the Coventry eastern by-pass in the 1970s, which effectively separated the premises from the city itself.

Much of the twin-engined Whitley bomber was assembled there during the 1930s and 1940s, but from 1948 onwards it was used exclusively for guided weapons' development. By the 1960s, however, the site was deserted, so in 1969 it was sold off to the Rootes Group (recently taken over by Chrysler of the USA). Rootes-Chrysler then redeveloped it as a motor-vehicle design and development technical centre, and concentrated all its new-model work at Whitley from 1970.

After Chrysler sold out to Peugeot in 1978, Whitley was controlled by Peugeot-Talbot Ltd; but that company then gradually ran down its new car design facilities, finally pulling out of Whitley and selling it on to Jaguar in 1985.

Jaguar then completely re-equipped the 155-acre site, built a sparkling new-style façade, erected several new buildings, made space for 1,000 engineers and their high-tech. equipment, and admitted to spending £55 million on the project. Technical staff began moving from Browns Lane to Whitley in 1987 and 1988, the complex being officially opened in May 1988.

Although XJ-S work was initially carried out at Browns Lane in the 1970s and 1980s, design and development work on the facelifted cars revealed in 1991 was completed at Whitley, as was the entire concept, design, development and proving of the XK8, which took over in 1996.

The new AJ-V8 engine was to become Jaguar's vitally important 'corporate' power unit in the 1990s and 2000s. It was first seen in 1996, just as the XK8 was ready to be launched.

Geoff Lawson was Jaguar's director of styling in the 1984–1999 period, when so many interesting new shapes were emerging from Jaguar. His design leader on the XK8 was Fergus Pollock.

approach. In 'building block' terms, a new car, which took up the project code of X100, would have nothing to do with the discredited XJ41/XJ42. That old car (even though it had never been brought to market, it was now very old, in terms of engineering and philosophy) would not be revised yet again, but would stay where it had already been consigned – to the dustbin of history.

In the first feet-on-the-table discussions, which came before any formal new model development, Jaguar considered several basic alternatives:

- Should the old, but still distinctive XJS, be put on life support by dropping the new V8 engine (*see* p.55)? This was effectively a sticking-plaster solution, soon discarded.
- Should the XJS be given a comprehensive front-end/tail-end facelift? This was certainly considered in sketches and mock-ups.
- Should the already mocked-up TWR coupé (which would become the Aston Martin DB7 of 1994) be taken up?
- Should an all-new style be adopted, with the new V8 engine to power it? This was always the favourite, and was always the basis of X100.

Looking back, styling manager Fergus Pollock later commented:

> We were asked initially to look at a £99 million facelift to the XJS. So we were asked to carry over the cabin and the doors, but to change the nose and tail – to make a new car out of it…but we couldn't make it work. There was simply too much XJS coming through, and the feeling was that it would be foolish to launch a car with a new engine, but with a body that resembled the last one.

It was out of this conundrum that one truly central decision was made, which would affect what the X100 could be, and what its developments would become in the years that followed: it would be based on the same basic floor-pan as the ageing XJS, and *not* on that of the current Jaguar XJ6/XJ12. Among the several very good and persuasive reasons for this was that Jaguar's planners thought they would be busy enough for a time with the new 'X300' saloons, without having to concern themselves with developing, and finding space for, a short-wheelbase version of the same platform.

Another very compelling reason was that when X100 was ready for launch, it would immediately take the place of the old XJS

Jaguar took over the Whitley Engineering Centre, on the eastern outskirts of Coventry, from Peugeot Talbot in the late 1980s, and the new XK8 would be totally designed, engineered and proven on this site. This view faces south, because the A45 Coventry by-pass highway is crossing the shot, behind the trees, at the top of the picture. Taken in 1987, this shows Whitley as Jaguar first occupied it. More buildings, and more new technology, would be added while the XK8 was being prepared.

Lovers of fine styling will surely recognize several 'cues' that carried over from this car – the limited-production XJ220 – into the XK8 that was to follow a few years later.

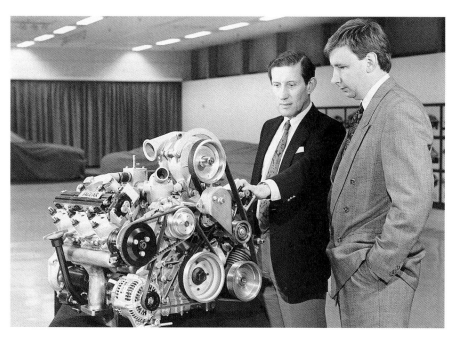

Was there ever any chance of Jaguar fitting this experimental two-stroke V6 engine into the XK8, after it had been revealed in 1992? Certainly not – as Trevor Crisp (who was totally in charge of all engine and transmission design and development at the time) made clear in later years. An interesting 'blind alley' project, though.

Although the new XK8 always looked exciting, the shape hid the most advanced Jaguar feature for years – the all-new 4-litre AJ-V8 engine.

range, which meant that the platform, some pressings, and the platform jigging for that car would suddenly be redundant, and available. That the forthcoming Aston Martin DB7 (*see* Appendix) would also use the same platform was a significant if not economically critical factor too.

So far, so good – and the designers (don't ever call a modern expert in this field a mere 'stylist' – he is considered to be much more capable that that!) could begin their work. The 'footprint' of the XJS – a 102in/2,591mm wheelbase, and front wheel tracks of around 59in/1,500mm (the latter figure would be about 1in (25mm) wider than the last of the XJSs) was therefore established, and all initial creative work could therefore be concentrated on the exterior style of the new car.

Apart from engineering the chassis of the new car, Jaguar also had to settle on the various trim packs with which they would launch the new car – these being the 'Classic' (top) and 'Sport' (bottom) trim packs.

Although Bob Dover eventually became chairman and chief executive of Jaguar and Land Rover, he rates the time when he led the engineering team who designed the XK8 as one of the most exciting times of his career.

Note that at this stage I wrote 'style', and not 'styles', because it wasn't immediately certain that there should be coupé and convertible types. On the other hand, it wasn't long before a study of current XJS sales' trends showed that the convertible was still the best seller, though both types were still in demand. Paradoxically, however, design studies concentrated on fixed-head coupé shapes at first.

New Shapes

First of all, a few names: Geoff Lawson had been director of the design/styling department both at Browns Lane since 1984 and at Whitley as soon as the department moved house (which means that he was also the man behind the scenes when the XJ41/XJ42 models were struggling to make their mark); but he left work on sports cars to Fergus Pollock, who would always be styling manager for this project. Martin Broomer ran the 'production planning' and

programme engineering side of the project at first – and would eventually be promoted to a public relations function.

At this point, and for clarity, I feel that I should start calling this new car the XK8 (its official name), and also make it clear that it was not the only badge considered. 'New XJS', 'XJ8' (there *was* no XJ8 saloon project at the time) and 'F-Type' were all considered. It was only when someone recalled that the E-Type had often been known as the XKE that XK-Eight began to sound reminiscent of what Jaguar was trying to achieve.

Although sketches were always being done (an artist spends much of his time sketching, this being a way of expressing himself), serious, formalized work on the new car did not begin until late 1991, when twenty-eight people began to concentrate their efforts. Geoff Lawson later insisted, persistently, that although the XK8 that was finalized had certain visual similarities to the Aston Martin DB7 (on which work was proceeding at the same time), the two cars were conceived quite separately and there was no co-operation between the teams. The DB7, let us be clear about this, was shaped at the TWR headquarters at Kidlington, near Oxford, under the control of Ian Callum.

In the early stages, Lawson set his team to work on four themes: two of their own (which they called 'Evocative' and 'Radical'), one from Ford's world studio at Dearborn, near Detroit, in the USA (this was the 'Progressive'), and a fourth from the Ghia studio in Italy ('Evolutionary') – Ghia was chosen because it was Ford's own 'skunk works' styling house, and the chief designer on that particular project was Moray Callum, who was Ian Callum's brother!

All these schemes progressed to the full-size clay model stage, and were painted up in silver, with five-spoke alloy road wheels. When door mirrors, grilles and headlamps/cowlings were added, these looked remarkably lifelike. Time was short (at the styling stage it always is), but somehow the four types were all ready for viewing, side by side, at Whitley, in March 1992. At that stage, all of them, without exception,

---

Ian Callum

Even if there had been no mechanical links between the Aston Martin DB7 and the Jaguar XK8 that followed it, Scottish-born designer Ian Callum would certainly have provided visual DNA links between the two cars, for he led the teams that shaped both cars.

Callum originally studied industrial design at the Glasgow School of Art, before moving on to specialize in automotive design at the Royal College of Art in London. From there he joined Ford, working his way through corporate design studios in Britain, Europe, Australia, Japan and the USA, before becoming design manager at Ford's Italian design subsidiary, Ghia Design Studios, in Turin. Then in 1990 he moved out of a large corporate atmosphere into a tiny workshop at TWR's headquarters in Kidlington, north of Oxford, which he later unkindly described thus: 'We had surface plates in there, a couple of offices, a little workshop, but no more…. I'd walked away from this giant studio at Dunton, the corporation, all that stuff, into this little tin shed.'

There he worked on the Jaguar-based TWR XX project that eventually evolved into the Aston Martin DB7, so it was inevitable that he should also direct work on the car that became the Jaguar XK8. Following the untimely death of Geoff Lawson, he then became Jaguar's Head of Design, those studios producing all later derivatives of the XK8, and of course the new-generation XK that took over in 2005.

---

were very rounded-looking offerings, with tails that dropped a little: the Dearborn offering had distinctly different left-hand and right-hand shapes, which gave even more choices.

Anyone who has worked in the motor industry knows that decisions taken at a management viewing can be very subjective. Individual directors – some of them not closely connected with the styling process, and others who may lack design expertise but have very flamboyant 'I know what I like' views – spend time pacing around the models before expressing an opinion. Sometimes such clays are exhibited indoors, and sometimes – though less often at the early stage – out of doors in what is usually called a 'styling garden'. In earlier periods, a management viewing at Jaguar was dominated, quite literally, by Sir William Lyons, who would have shaped the car himself and merely wanted to double-check his judgement; by the 1990s, however, collective responsibility had taken over – and would sometimes delay matters significantly.

Surprisingly, the Ford-Dearborn offering fell at almost the first hurdle, because its straight-through wing crown line and its pure hatchback rear style were not liked. This left the other three different styles – the two Jaguar styles and the one from Ghia – which were to be further developed.

By June 1992 the three surviving clay models had all been refined and were ready for a further viewing, to take account of comments and recommendations made by Jaguar experts in departments as various as product planning (how did the new stack up against the opposition, and against the older XKS?), production engineering (how could the cars be made?), engineering feasibility (could they be screwed together conveniently?), or legislation (would the cars meet the latest/projected regulations for things such as crash testing, driver visibility, air bag installations?).

This time round the two Jaguar proposals survived and went through to the next stage, but the Ghia offering was reluctantly discarded. Perhaps just a shade too anonymous for the prevailing management team, it gave way to Jaguar's own offerings, leaving the Ghia team to go back and pick up the next Ford 'skunk works' project; they were disappointed, certainly, but knew that this was the way such decisions were often made.

Almost immediately afterwards, each of the Jaguar clays – 'Evocative' and Radical' – had their clay skinned in a thin plastic film, then painted to look almost eerily like a real car. They were then flown to California, and shown under strictly controlled conditions to a party of what Jaguar called 'target customers', who might buy such a new car, or maybe a Mercedes-Benz SL500, or the latest in Lexus models.

At this point a gap appeared between the two types: what Jaguar always described as 'Radical' was not universally received, possibly because its headlamp and tail-lamp clusters looked rather less practical than they might, and possibly because it did not feature the famous Jaguar 'haunches' above and behind the rear wheel-arch cut-outs. Interestingly, enough 'Evocative' featured those haunches, and also more practical lamp fittings, which may explain why the public seemed to like it so much. Other clinics held in other locations confirmed the same impressions.

Even so, this car still featured a traditional type of Jaguar saloon-car grille (the sort that would eventually reappear on the S-Type saloon of 1998), although it would shortly be discarded. By the autumn of 1992 'Evocative' ('evocative' of the E-Type, Geoff Lawson thought, and very different indeed from the outgoing XJS) had become the firm favourite, in fact so much so that the styling office produced several other variations on the theme – these included a wide-mouth grille, and the truncation of the tail (which would be shortened by 6in/150mm), thereby allowing the familiar outline of the XK8 tail-lamps to emerge. This chop, incidentally, would be quite costly, because it would mean making changes to the rear end of the XJS platform, which was still set to be retained, but now in more modified form than ever.

According to Jaguar legend, the truly important date came on 10 October 1992. Two final clays, known as 'A' and 'M', were shown to 300 carefully selected prospective customers at a clinic at the National Exhibition Centre in Birmingham. Both, of course, were coupés, because the convertible style was still not ready, even though doctored photographs and rendering were also available at the time. This was the final proof that Lawson's team needed, because 'A', complete with the shorter tail, was well liked (particularly in convertible form); moreover a further last-minute clinic in Los Angeles, California, confirmed that judgement.

By this time, too, the 'packaging engineers' had been working away at proposals for the new car's interior. Knowing that the ageing XJS was sometimes criticized for having a less-than-spacious cabin, every opportunity was taken to enlarge that of the new car. In the end, Pollock's exterior design team (who had always worked in concord with the packaging experts) managed to push the windscreen forwards by no less than 7in/175mm, and the rear window was set further back than it had been on the XJS (there were no flying buttresses to accommodate, after all) – and the rest was a matter of concentrating on fractions.

Once again, Geoff Lawson had telling comments to make: 'V8 engines are shorter than straight sixes, so it made sense to physically shorten the XK8's bonnet. That, in turn, allowed us to move the base of the windscreen 7 inches further forwards.' Because the roof was marginally higher and more rounded than before, it all helped.

Building the First Cars

Once Jaguar's then chairman, ex-Ford man Nick Scheele, had signed off the style and told the team to get on with it as rapidly as possible, a concentrated multi-car programme had to swing into action. As we later found out, between 1993 and 1996 more than 130 prototypes, or pilot-build machines, had to be built before series manufacture could begin. Although the XK8's platform was modified XJS, and many of the suspension and steering components were carryovers from other Jaguar models, almost everything else was destined to be new – engine, automatic transmission, body shell, and all the passenger amenities including new air conditioning, facia/instrument fittings and many other details.

A tough, resourceful and experienced engineer was needed to take this project forwards – from X100 to XK8, in fact. To Ford's eternal credit they did not search around within their own empire, but moved swiftly and decisively close to home at Jaguar, and appointed Bob

When the XK8 was developed, there was never any doubt that original cars would all have a 'traditionally British' type of facia/instrument panel, including pillar-to-pillar wood, and with the familiar Jaguar 'J-gate' type of automatic transmission selector on the centre console.

Bob Dover

No one ever accused Bob Dover of being a shrinking violet, for wherever the XK8 was discussed, Dover tended to be the personality wheeled out to talk about the car, and to explain what had been done in the years since he became Jaguar's chief programme engineer, sports cars. Normally Jaguar's industrial parent company, Ford, did not encourage personalities, but in this case they made an exception.

Originally starting his working life as an apprentice at RAE Farnborough in 1962, he moved rapidly up through the ranks as a hands-on engineer. By 1968 he was a project engineer at the Pressed Steel body operation of British Leyland in the Midlands; then in 1976 he moved out of cars and into tractors, at Massey Ferguson, where he worked all round the world, notably in the USA, South Africa, Poland and France.

Finally he returned to Land Rover as manufacturing director in the 1980s, became project director on the original Discovery 4×4, and joined Jaguar in 1986 as manufacturing director. Having steered the XK8 on to the market, he would go on to become Jaguar's CEO, then was further promoted to become chairman of Jaguar Land Rover, before retiring in the early 2000s.

Dover as chief programme engineer. In a way, this was an all-can-do title that summed everything up perfectly; no matter when, how or why, or from which direction, for the next three years the buck always stopped in front of Bob Dover.

Although one styling clay after another had been built, assessed, rejected, approved and discussed before then, it wasn't until the first XJS-shelled 'simulators' went on to the road, and the merits of the new 'AJ26' V8 engine became clear, that Bob Dover started to look less than harassed; in his words: 'April/May 1993 – that is probably the earliest we all felt comfortable about it. Well, comfortable enough to put our careers on the line, anyhow.'

But before the XK8 was ready for production, there were several distinct phases of design and development, and this is where I must descend once again to 'Jaguar-speak'. First of all the style (already described) had to be settled, and then the mechanical engineering. And

Immediately before launch, Jaguar sent a production-standard XK8 coupé out on to the banking of a test track where it was just able to show off its 150mph (240km/h)-plus top speed…

…even though no transverse rear spoiler was fitted to control the car's stability at such high speeds.

even while this was going on, a series of simulator cars (basically, these were progressively and increasingly modified XJS types, with some XK8 features being tested) had to be produced, after which mechanical prototypes – still looking much like familiar XJSs, but with XK8 running gear hidden away under the skin – followed. The first cars looking like XK8s were to be the evaluation prototypes, and finally, when all testing had confirmed the appropriate specification, a series of verification prototypes would be needed.

Prototypes and Test Cars

In three years, Jaguar produced more than 130 prototypes dedicated to the X100/XK8 programme:

Simulators: Between October 1992 and October 1993, twenty-four cars, mostly based on XJS coupés and convertibles, were built up to test components, mainly engines and other proposed mechanical components. Of these cars, three were hybrids with XK8 front ends grafted on to XJS structures, with V8 engines, and were subjected to frontal crash testing; two others were 'half-and-half' XJS/XJ8 body shells, and were subjected to side crash testing; and one 'car' was a full size XK8 body shell in glass fibre, used for wind-tunnel evaluation.

Mechanical prototypes: Between September 1993 and July 1994 (and with one further car finally completed in December 1994), forty-six cars were completed, many of them using XJS coupé and convertible body shells, but with complete XK8 running gear including V8 engines, ZF transmissions and the latest suspension fittings. Of these, no fewer than ten had hybrid, but mechanically and structurally appropriate, XK8-shaped body shells, and were subjected to further crash testing – five front end, and five side-on impacts.

Evaluation prototypes: Between October 1994 and April 1995 – a very compressed period indeed – twenty-nine more cars were completed, these being the first batch of cars that looked like, and structurally were like, the XK8 that would eventually be launched. Because the robot assembly line was sourced in Japan, Jaguar actually had thirty bodies-in-white built out there, using British steel, so that the entire installation could be adjusted and proven before being shipped to the UK.

Although completion of work on the convertible – especially of the silkily efficient soft-top operation – was running some months behind that of the coupé, coupés and convertibles were used for every aspect of the testing and – literally – the 'evaluation' process, to be sure the machine that had been designed and engineered on computers, and in the design studios, behaved as was hoped, and expected, in real life.

During 1995 two of these cars – a coupé and a convertible – were shipped to the USA in conditions of great secrecy, where they were tested and assessed by Jaguar North America (JNA) top management. After their return they were sent to Scotland, where no less than triple F1 World Champion Jackie Stewart (who was a hard-working vehicle behaviour consultant to Ford at this time) tried both cars.

Once again, several cars of this batch reached a violent end, two of them being subjected to front and rear crash tests respectively, and two more to side-on crash testing, too.

Verification prototypes: This was the final testing phase, when cars that had all been assembled around the first 'pilot build' off-tools body shells, under production line conditions, were produced to make finally sure that the project was ready for launch. In another very concentrated period – September 1995 to January 1996 – thirty-three cars were built. This time the carnage due to crash testing was even more intense, for no fewer than ten cars (four of them convertibles) were ruthlessly hurled into concrete blocks to confirm that they met all known test requirements.

Some cars went off to Timmins in Canada for harsh weather winter testing and verification, and others went to Arizona for hot weather testing. The last two to be built were the coupé, unveiled at Geneva in March 1996, and the convertible, first shown at the New York Auto Show in April.

It was only then that serious work on the XKR – which would not be launched for a further two years – could get under way.

Mean, moody and…XK8, a car that looked completely different from the XJS that it replaced in 1996.

By any previous Jaguar standards, this was going to be a huge programme, and the (compressed) list opposite shows just how many cars/mock-ups or body shells were involved: twenty-four simulators, forty-six mechanical prototypes, twenty-nine evaluation prototypes and no fewer than thirty-three verification prototypes. Not that all these would ever been seen in public, for a number would be ruthlessly put through the mandatory crash test procedures, and others would not venture outside the laboratories, workshops or design studios.

The New V8 Engine

Even before the first styling lines took shape in the studios at Whitley, there was one absolutely crucial decision to be taken: what engine, or choice of engines, should be used in the new XK8? After all, engines were massive 'building

blocks', and expensive to design and build, too – and their bulk was bound to govern the shape and profile of the panels surrounding the engine bay: for packaging, cost and engineering reasons, these would have to be wrapped as closely and carefully around the engine assembly as possible.

For Jaguar in the early 1990s, there was never going to be a simple answer to this conundrum, and the search went on for a long time. It was not a new search, either – as my survey of the complicated history of the XJ41/XJ42 has just made clear. As Trevor Crisp (at the time Jaguar's group chief engineer, engines and transmissions) told me at a later date:

The new 6-cylinder AJ6 [as chosen for use in XJ41/XJ42] was nearly ready when I took over – Harry Mundy and Ron Burr, between them, had designed it. But the long-term strategy had been very unclear. After the V12 had come in, and the V8 version of that engine had been thrown out, work started on a slant-six instead. But at 2.7 litres, it wasn't going to be powerful enough.

Under Geoffrey Robinson [who was Jaguar's Chairman in the mid-1970s after 'Lofty' England retired] Jaguar had also done a new 4-valve head on the old cast-iron XK block, then a new block, and then there was an aluminium block. Eventually that was dropped, the alternative AJ6 heads – 2-valve and 4-valve – came along, the size went up to 3.6 litres, and that was virtually finalized when I took over. There was certainly a lot going on at this time, but not much of it reached the public.

Late in the 1980s, and with future saloons also in mind, Jaguar quite naturally wanted to design a completely new engine of its own. But in view of what has just been explained, was there still any viable life and potential in the development of existing engines? Soon after it took control, and because it always claimed to have a global outlook, the parent company, Ford, ordered that a world-wide survey of *all* the Ford Corporation's current and proposed engines – British, European, North American and even Pacific Rim power units – should be made. Was it even necessary, Ford asked, that Jaguar should design yet another engine, if something suitable already existed somewhere else in the world? Raising production of an existing engine would be economically viable, and because of the huge saving in capital spending, the cost of shipping engines from one continent to another was a tiny consideration.

When work began on the new car that would become XK8, the survey, and the decisions that followed, had already been made – but the way in which this was done deserves study. At the time, of course, all existing Jaguars were powered by one or other of the 6-cylinder AJ6 power units, or with the ageing and thirsty V12 engine – both of which fitted neatly into the engine bay that would form a template for the new body shell. Neither, however, was likely to be suitable for X100, for the following reasons.

Trevor Crisp

Although it was Bob Dover and his team who gained most of the publicity surrounding the new XK8, it was Trevor Crisp and his engine design colleagues who must take all the credit for the V8 engine, which was the absolute heart and soul of the new model. Like the author, Trevor Crisp started his career as a student at Brown's Lane in the 1950s; he then worked his way up through the engineering hierarchy, and notched up forty-five years of service with Jaguar, before Ford moved him across to be Cosworth's managing director until 2001, when he retired.

Having completed his traineeships, Trevor became the engine design and development engineer in the 1960s, learned much about exhaust emissions, and moved up to be chief engine development engineer in 1977. Three years after that, when his mentor, Harry Mundy, retired, Trevor also took over responsibility for transmissions, drive lines and cooling system installations.

In the next two decades Trevor's team finalized, and evolved, and made a big success out of the AJ6/AJ16 6-cylinder engine; they also completed the final developments of the famous V12 engine (including much non-publicized work on 4-valve twin-cam versions for TWR's race cars), and the experimental two-stroke engine that was seen once – and once only. They also devised, developed and refined the AJ-V8 power unit.

Although Trevor retired in 2001, he stayed in touch with all his old colleagues, and at the time of writing he was still an active member of the 'Ex-Apprentices' group, of which the author is also proud to be a member.

First, by this time the venerable V12 engine was living on borrowed time. Designed in the 1960s, in production from 1971, and due to be finally enlarged from 5.3 litres to 6 litres in 1993 for the last of the XJS types, it was a phenomenally smooth and torquey power unit and magnificent to behold – but it was expensive to manufacture and had a well deserved reputation for high fuel consumption. Not only that, but Jaguar's engineers could see no way of making it comply with USA exhaust emission legislation that would apply from

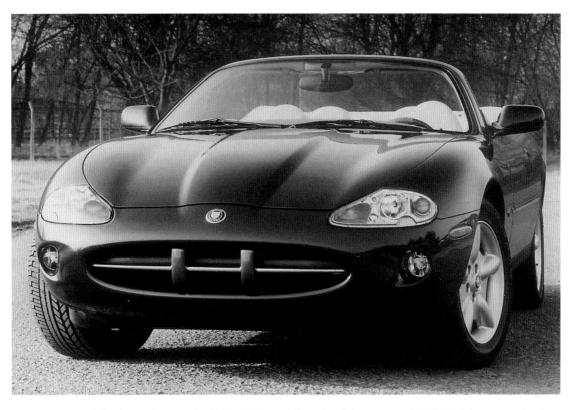

Because Jaguar needed to be sure that even the 400bhp XKR would be well cooled, every type of XK8 (this being a conventional, normally aspirated convertible) had a large and shapely front air intake. No bumper, of course, though what we might describe as 'over-riders' were to be found close to the centre of the grille.

1996, which meant that it must soon be phased out.

Second, although the 6-cylinder AJ6 – soon to become the more powerful and more efficient AJ16 in 1994, in the last of the XJS types – was a fine engine, it also seemed to have been around for a long time. It was also what engineers liked to admit was a 'mature' design, meaning, basically, that there was little more positive development still to come, though at the time it was used in many Jaguar and Daimler saloons as well as the ageing XJS. It had already had a long life. Launched in 1983 as a 24-valve 3.6-litre, it eventually spawned versions as different as a 12-valve single-cam 2.9-litre and a 24-valve 4-litre twin-cam, while a supercharged version had just been chosen to power the still-secret Aston Martin

DB7. Amazingly, however, no 6-cylinder-powered XJS would go on sale in North America until 1993. So once again, here was an engine that had already been extended and expanded to its practical limits, so if the new X100 model was to have a distinguished long life it would have to be powered by something else, something more modern, and with much development potential.

The worldwide survey requested by Ford had not produced any encouraging results, for the 'empire' was not exactly overendowed with engines that could produce 300bhp in normally aspirated form, and up to 400bhp for ultra-sporting types (of which the still-under-discussion XKR would be typical). In fact, except for one new type of V8 being developed by Ford in North America, and produced

57

Jaguar was one of the very first car makers to use ZF's state-of-the-art, five-speed automatic transmission, which was mated to the new V8 engine and fitted to the XK8 and other Jaguars in the late 1990s. It gave exemplary service. Later, from 2002, it was supplanted by a six-speed ZF transmission instead.

at the engine plant at Romeo, in Michigan USA, a brisk search round the worldwide empire did not turn up any other startling and obvious power units that might be suitable.

Even so, and to this day, there are those who suggested that Jaguar was hasty in rejecting this new engine – the 99F/Romeo – which had been newly launched for use in the 1990 Lincoln Town Car (and later used in other big Fords and Lincolns). For interest, therefore, I quote the main characteristics, which were:

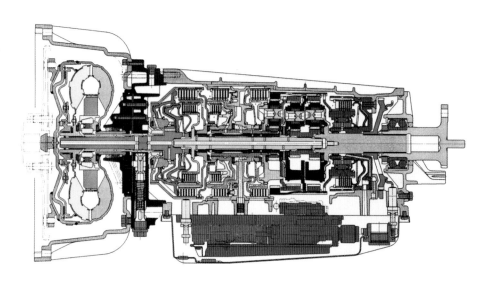

Like the Mercedes-Benz automatic transmission that would be fitted to XKR models (see Chapter 5), the ZF transmission fitted to the XK8 was a compact and efficient transmission unit.

Edging towards a solution: this was one of the styling scale models of the early 1990s, which eventually led to the finalized shape of the XK8 model.

At one point in the early 1990s, there was even a proposal to prolong the life of the ageing XJS by providing it with a new nose and front-end style. Nothing came of it.

- 90-degree V8, (bore and stroke) 90.2 × 90mm, 4601cc
- 2 valves per cylinder, single overhead camshaft per cylinder bank
- 192bhp at 4,200rpm, or 212bhp at 4,600rpm

It was not, in other words, engineered to the same level of sophistication as an engine that Jaguar might want to use, and it was certainly not powerful enough at the outset. Seven years on, in fairness, Ford USA also produced a much-improved twin-cam version, with four valves per cylinder, for the latest Lincoln Continental, but even that engine produced only 279bhp at 5,750rpm. Even so, it was clearly not in the same performance league as Jaguar's own offering.

Jaguar's engineers, of course, knew all about this, for they always kept a careful lookout for what their rivals were doing. Accordingly, work was already going on, behind closed doors, on a new generation of engines – originally only at the drawing board/computer stage. As Trevor Crisp recalls:

> Way back, the general idea was that we would have a new generation of engines – not just the V8 that you know, but closely related V6 and V12 types, too. We would have built them on new tooling, at the Radford factory, with 60-degree V6 and V12s, and a 90-degree V8. That was the plan for a long time – we had designed the original V8 in, I think, 1987, and done some work on the V6 and V12 derivatives before Ford took over. That would have covered every requirement, from less than 3 litres, all the way to 6 litres.
>
> The arrival of Ford, however, caused a big hiccup in the programme for, as already stated, Ford wanted to make a full review of everything that was being proposed, and how every project might – or might not, in some cases – make economic sense, and fit in with other new project work that Ford (and to a less critical extent, Aston Martin) was considering.
>
> Ford's review team was led by Jaguar's new managing director, Bill Hayden, who was a real pussy cat then, but that soon changed…. He soon

killed off most of the grandiose and impractical suggestions. In particular, this team kicked out the proposed V6 and V12 projects.

> [We now know, of course, that Ford was already working on a new V6 project of its own – an evolution of which would eventually be used in Jaguar S-Type and X-Type models – and that a V12 engine that was related to that V6 would be re-engineered by Cosworth, and fitted to late 1990s Aston Martins.]
>
> Clive Ennos arrived from Ford to replace Jim Randle. Clive was so enthusiastic, so 'sold' on Jaguar, that we couldn't have asked for more. Bill Hayden encouraged us to get the new V8 petrol engine running, though there were times when we were under great pressure to use the new 'Romeo' all-aluminium 4.6-litre V8 from Ford-USA instead. It was a great engine, but it was physically too big – and it wasn't a Jaguar.
>
> In the end he approved of our new V8, but not the V6 or the V12 that we wanted to add to the family, especially as that would have involved using different cylinder block and crankshaft machinery for different cylinder bank angles. In fact we never even made any V6 or V12 prototypes. Eventually, too, everyone was impressed by the performance of the supercharged V8, and that was seen to negate the need for a V12 after all.
>
> It was always obvious to me that, for Jaguar, a supercharger was a better solution than a turbocharger – we did that with the help of Eaton, and brought it in without needing to make any body-shell modification. Initial sales projections, by the way, were very low – it was thought to be worth a 5 per cent take-up – and in the end sales were up to 15 per cent.

In the end, therefore, the new AJ-V8 engine matured into a compact 90-degree power unit. With twin camshafts per bank (chain-driven from the nose of the crankshaft), four valves per cylinder and with light alloy castings for cylinder block and the heads, it was at once state of the art, but was an engine designed for a long life, and to meet every known (and even projected) exhaust emission and noise test regulation with which a modern car concern was faced. At the prototype stage, incidentally, cylinder-head castings were provided by Cosworth from its ultra-modern foundry in Worcester: Cosworth was renowned for its work on such castings, and had previously worked on Jaguar-type V12s as used by the TWR-Jaguar race team.

For the XK8, normally aspirated varieties had Japanese Nippondenso fuel injection and engine management systems, while the supercharged derivative also had a slim, but effective, Roots-type Eaton supercharger, neatly positioned in the cylinder V, and belt-driven from the nose of the crankshaft.

As originally launched, the cylinder bore and stroke of the AJ-V8 both measured 86mm, and while Jaguar staff would confirm nothing, it was tacitly admitted that there was a little bit of 'stretch' built in, to allow for future enlargements. As we now know (this is made clear in the chart shown on p. 65), the engine could eventually be enlarged to at least 4.4 litres.

All in all, the new power unit had a lot to live up to, because it was, in all fairness, only the fourth all-new power unit that Jaguar had ever put on sale since 1945 – the 6-cylinder XK, the V12, and the 6-cylinder AJ6 being the others. All had built their own magnificent reputations for power, torque, longevity, refinement and tunability – and that other indefinable feature that we will merely describe as 'character'.

But where would Jaguar make this all-new engine? Was it not logical that the new AJ-V8 should be manufactured and assembled at the ex-Daimler factory in Radford, which was now Jaguar's power house? This factory, after all, had once been Daimler's main assembly plant, had been a part of the Jaguar 'empire' since 1960, and after decades of rationalization was producing nothing but engines, transmission and some suspension assemblies. By the early 1990s both existing Jaguar engines – AJ6/AJ16 and the V12 power unit – were being built there, although in truth, by Ford standards, the plant was somewhat under-used and in need of modernization and further investment.

Bridgend Factory

Starting from a green-field site on the eastern outskirts of Bridgend in South Wales, Ford developed an all-new factory in the late 1970s to build new-generation overhead-camshaft CVH 4-cylinder engines for front-wheel-drive Escorts and Fiestas. First commissioned in mid-1980, the Bridgend engine plant soon became a vital part of Ford's European manufacturing empire, and has been expanding ever since.

By the late 1980s Bridgend was producing more than 2,000 CVH engines a day, after which an additional manufacturing facility was erected to allow the manufacture of 16-valve Zetec 4-cylinder engines for new Escort and Mondeo models, of which assembly would continue until 2004. More than six million CVH and 3.6 million Zetec types of all types were produced.

Ford then approved the design of the Jaguar V8 engine that powered all XK8 types and was later to be fitted to S-Type and XJ-type saloons, and it erected yet another factory extension at Bridgend to make these engines. The very first Jaguar V8s were produced at Bridgend in 1996, the range soon being expanded to include supercharged variants; by the early 2000s the range also included 4.2-litre and 4.4-litre types, which were also fitted to upmarket Land Rover Discovery and Range Rover types.

By this time Bridgend was an incredibly versatile operation. Since 1980, CVHs had given way to Zetecs, Zetecs had given way to smaller, lighter and more efficient Zetec SEs, and from 2006 an all-new straight-six engine for Land Rover and Volvo was also added to the corporate range.

By 2005, well over half-a-million engines a year (of which more than 60,000 were AJ-V8 types for Jaguar and Land Rover) were being produced, and with further manufacturing updates planned, Ford claimed they would be able to build up to a million engines every year from 2010. Although Ford sold Jaguar (and Land Rover) to Tata in 2008, it was thought that the engine supply deal was safe for some years to come.

One of many steps along the road to getting the X100 theme refined and ready for approval by management. At this time the sides of the style still lacked detail definition, and more work needed to be done on tail lamp/rear bumper/moulding themes.

Since the V12 engine was due to go out of production in 1997 – there was neither the will, nor the technical ability to stretch its life even further – and the AJ16 'six' would follow suit at the same time, the old transfer line machinery could therefore become a prime candidate for clearing away, and a lot of empty factory space would be exposed in this ex-aircraft component factory. Surely the AJ-V8 could slot in there perfectly?

Ford, though, had other ideas. Down in South Wales, and close to Bridgend, since the late 1970s they had been developing an enormous, super-efficient and well financed factory dedicated purely to engine manufacture, on a huge scale. Having started in 1980 with the building of overhead-camshaft 4-cylinder engines for use in new-generation front-wheel-drive Escorts, Bridgend later moved on to produce even more modern power units – and plenty of ground space for further extensions still existed.

By the early 1990s Ford had decided to build the new Jaguar V8 engines on the extended Bridgend site, and one immediate consequence was that, in Coventry, the Radford factory became redundant, and was razed to the ground at the end of the 1990s.

According to Ford, no less than $165 million (Ford always talks in dollars – let's guess at about £90 million in sterling) was invested in new facilities wrapped around the existing plant. Some of the individual costs are staggering – they included $27.3/£15 million for cylinder head machining tools, $27.5/£15 million for the block and $22.3/£12.4 million for the crankshaft. Not only that, but provision had already been made for 4.0-litre (XK8) and 3.2-litre (later XJ saloons) sizes – and as we know, several other sizes have been added to the list since the original launch.

The first off-tools AJ-V8s were manufactured in 1995, series production built up rapidly ahead of the launch of the sporty Jaguar in the autumn of 1996, and over the years the rate of production built up steadily, especially when derivatives of this power unit were specified for the latest generation Land Rovers and Range Rovers.

In 1992, what became known as 'Clay 2' was one of two favoured themes in the internal styling competition, but was eventually discarded. It was noted for what I will now call the 'S-Type' front grille, while there were a number of different attempts at the positioning of side/turn indicator lamps to match this.

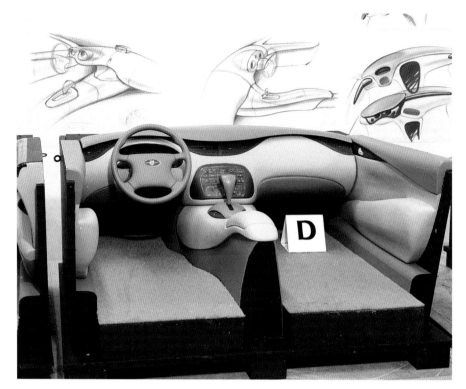

In the early stages, any number of full-size mock-ups were made of potential facia/ instrument panel layouts. This was the most avant garde of all, and was soon dismissed by the traditionalists in top management...

...but this is much nearer the final style. The actual wheel/ instrument/centre console position is nearly there, but the colour and finish is still to be chosen.

The New V8 Engine

It always happens. A new generation of Jaguar V8 engine, originally built only in 4-litre form, gradually evolved into a complete family, and by the mid-2000s was being used in several Jaguar and Range Rover models. When JLR was sold off to the Tata Group in 2008, it seemed as if this V8 would nevertheless be an important 'building block' in Jaguar's line-up for some time to come.

Details of this engine's development are included in the main text, but here is a summary of the way the family evolved:

Cubic Capacity (cc)	Bore × stroke (mm)	First used in	Original power rating
3253	86 × 70	XJ8 saloon, 1997	237bhp
3555	86 × 76.5	XJ saloon, 2002	258bhp
3996	86 × 86	XK8, 1996	290bhp
4196	86 × 90.3	XK8, 2002	300bhp
4394	88 × 90.3	Range Rover Sport, 2004	299bhp

Furthermore, when this book was originally drafted in 2008, there were unconfirmed stories about a 5-litre derivative being developed for Range Rover usage.

Transmission

Right from the start, Jaguar's product planners concluded that although their policy was so well honed and successful on the long-running XJS range, there was no longer any coherent demand for manual transmission in a new sporty Jaguar with so much power and torque. In the 1980s and 1990s, a five-speed (German) Getrag manual transmission had been available with the 6-cylinder XJS models, but had not sold widely. From 1979, in any case, all V12-engined Jaguars had only been supplied with automatic transmission. Jaguar customers, it seemed, now wanted an automatic transmission to do all the ratio-changing for them.

But which particular automatic transmission should it be? If Jaguar had still been an independent concern, the planners would have had less of a problem in making a choice. But in the 1990s the options were distinctly limited. Earlier V12-engined XJS types had used the General Motors GM400 transmission with three forward ratios, while for the 6-litre V12-engined cars that had been replaced by a

further evolution, the General Motors four-ratio GM 4L80-E was used instead.

That was all very well, and there was no technical problem – the 4L80-E transmission was, after all, also considered good enough for Rolls-Royce to use it at this time too – but there was now a major political problem. For all the obvious industrial reasons, Ford-USA did not consider it possible for a GM transmission to be used in a Jaguar – for GM was Ford's major competitor, world-wide. In addition, and for marketing reasons, a five-speed transmission was now considered desirable.

Because of the amount of power and torque that was to be standardized – especially in supercharged form – the problem was to find an alternative. Nothing was available from within the Ford-USA empire (not even the transmission fitted to massive-engined Lincolns was considered adequate), but fortunately Jaguar was able to turn to ZF of Germany for advice and supplies.

ZF, a very experienced and very well thought-of supplier of automatics, already built several different models in several sizes and torque capacities (one of their principal and

Which side would Sir prefer? In many cases, a studio-prepared full-size clay model would have differing sides around a longitudinal centre line. The right side of this clay had elliptical headlamps and quite a high grille, while the left side is about to have the definitive headlamp shape, and a front grille rather closer to the ground.

Every picture tells a story, and in this case – what a story! As posed in 1992, here are (left to right) a final XJ41, an early X100 Clay (Clay 1 – ex-Ghia Studio) and a late model XJS.

most valued clients was BMW), and one of their four-speed units was already being used by Jaguar in the 4-litre/6-cylinder-engined XJS. Even when the XK8 was originally planned, ZF let it be known that they were developing a new generation of five-speed transmissions, and that one of these could be suitable for use behind the new V8 engine.

Because such a five-speed ZF transmission would already be in series production by the time Jaguar needed it (BMW was already planning to use it by the mid-1990s), there would be no worries about employing new and rather unproven technology. Accordingly, Jaguar made the choice – and would also use the same box in the forthcoming XJ8 saloon car range, too. Even so, and as we shall see when the time comes to describe the supercharged XKR, not even this new transmission would be right for every possible application – but that decision would have to be made in the future!

Chassis Development and Testing

Now the testing had to begin. No matter what experience told them regarding older models, the team could not yet be sure that the first XK8s to be built would heave in the way that they hoped. The only way to make sure was to build up the cars, build up the mileage, and sort out the wrinkles.

With the choice of engine and transmissions now made, Bob Dover's team could turn to the many other aspects that had to be tackled to turn 'good idea' into 'job done'. The fact that the XK8 would use the same basic floor-pan as the XJS, and that there was already much synergy between sporty Jaguars and Jaguar saloons, meant that much suspension, steering and braking expertise continued to evolve.

Although it would be easy to summarize the underpinnings of the XK8 – coil spring independent front suspension, coil spring independent rear suspension, four-wheel disc brakes, and power-assisted rack-and-pinion steering – and assume that there were no improvements, that would be quite wrong.

Much detail – by which I mean thousands of man-hours of detail work – went into advancing innovations, especially those connected with making the new car stronger, more reliable and more refined than ever before.

Purely as an example, for cost reasons Jaguar would have liked to carry forwards the sturdy, steel, XJS front suspension cross-member, but at the computer layout stage they discovered that this member would always want to occupy the same space as the sump pan of the new AJ-V8 engine. To redesign the V8 engine sump would be to deprive it of oil capacity and bring further complications, so instead Jaguar treated the XK8 to a new and rather tortuously shaped die-cast aluminium cross-member instead – one that carried front suspension mountings, steering rack mountings *and* the front engine mountings. It also proved to be 13lb/6kg lighter than the old XJS member.

Less work was needed around the rear suspension area, for much of the basic layout, if not the detailing, came from the latest high-powered XJR four-door saloon. Like all modern Jaguars of the period, this featured fixed-length drive shafts as part of the suspension geometry.

More time, and more effort, would go into getting other details right, which is why certain prototypes were dedicated totally to, say, air-conditioning development, to brake testing, to traction control development, to airbag sensor calibration, and more.

In a much more concentrated way than they had ever worked with earlier models, Jaguar tested the XK8 more widely, more intensively and more severely than ever before. To get at the extremes, they established a hot climate engineering centre at Lone Cactus Drive, Phoenix, Arizona (think 'Death Valley', 122°F/ 50°C in the sunshine in mid-August, and if it was sheer blistering heat you wanted, you wouldn't be far wrong), and a winter centre at Timmins, in Canada, where temperatures regularly plumbed the depths of –40°F/–40°C. Timmins, incidentally, was no small place, but well off any normal tourist's beaten track, north of the Great Lakes, but still not too far from Ottowa and Toronto.

The programme took time to get under way, but once in full swing was active all round the world, all the time. Timmins, naturally, went into hibernation during Canada's summer, the Arizona facility was no warmer than a British summer during the 'depths' of a Phoenix winter, while Jaguar drew on specialist facilities – such as the super-high-speed testing bowl at Nardo, way down in the heel of Italy, when ultimate performance needed to be checked out. It was at Nardo, incidentally, that one of the very first spy-camera shots was taken, for where top speeds had to be verified, then the car had to be run in a fully-equipped, open-to-scrutiny condition.

The testing of simulators and mechanical prototypes was easier to manage because most of the cars looked like rather down-at-heel XJSs, but evaluation prototypes were based on the first XK8 shells and needed more disguise when out in public. The very first all-metal, all-XK8-shape coupé (EP8) ran in November 1994 and took twenty-one days to build up, whereas the second, a convertible, EP33, took only eleven days. Jaguar's XK8 project team were becoming more and more expert as time went along, and at the same time prototype supplies were becoming more easily available.

Even so, this was a big programme for a relatively small company such as Jaguar to accommodate. Unlike Ford of Europe (which had substantial 'pilot plants' to produce early runs of what I call 'shake-down' models – the

British one being at Aveley/South Ockendon, in Essex), Jaguar had to make do with more modest facilities. In the winter of 1994/1995 the first evaluation prototypes, and the very first verification prototypes, were assembled on what was known as 'Track Seven' at Browns Lane, where casual factory visitors were not allowed to penetrate.

Towards the end of 1995, when the XJS was still in series production (but the entire world seemed to know that its end was near), twenty-nine of the VPs, in 'almost-there' condition, were put together on the main assembly line. For even the most died-in-the-wool assembly workers, this must have been an exciting time, for some of them had been building nothing except XJSs for well over a decade – and now they found the very first examples of the new car coming along.

Not that everything always went according to plan. One of the mechanical prototypes was written off in a rear-end collision in Pheonix, Arizona, two of the evaluation prototypes were damaged at the MIRA test track in 1995, another suffered rear-end damage out on the open road close to the factory, while yet another suffered when it was damaged in Jaguar's own experimental workshops at Whitley. The last little contretemps was the most embarrassing of all – but all four cars were repaired and put back into use.

By March 1996, every possible button had been pushed, every possible sign-off document had been approved, and the XK8 was ready for launch. What would the public think of it?

4 The XK8 on Sale – the Early Years

Like other companies in the Ford empire in the 1990s, Jaguar was encouraged to show off its new models, and to give them an official preview, months before deliveries could actually begin. This required a certain amount of confidence in their potential customers' patience – and a prediction that sales of the old model (which was usually still on sale) would not fall away the moment this was done.

This explains, no doubt, that although the XK8 was launched in a flurry of publicity at the Geneva Motor Show in March 1996, the first customer cars did not reach their lucky owners until the autumn of the same year. In the USA, the first cars would not be delivered until the very beginning of 1997. As the old model, the XJS, was to come to the end of its twenty-one-year career at Browns Lane in April 1996, in fact this was no embarrassment.

As all the new car's technicalities have been described in the previous chapter, it is now time to concentrate on the car's reception in

Two versions of the XK8 were launched in the spring of 1996, this being the convertible version.

When the power-operated soft-top of the XK8 was erect, the interior could be as snug as that of the fixed-head coupé.

The original XK8 Convertible was a very handsome car, especially with the hood folded back and concealed by its cover. Do you remember when cars used to have front and rear bumpers? Not the XK8, though.

1996, and on the way that Jaguar ushered it into British showrooms before the end of that year. Thanks to invaluable information provided by Anders Clausager of the Jaguar Daimler Heritage Trust, it is now known that just twenty 'pilot build' cars had officially been completed on the regular assembly lines in 1995 – eight coupés and twelve convertibles – and that Job 1 (which is industry-speak for 'the start-up of real volume production') came in June 1996. To bowdlerize Winston Churchill's famous aphorism about the production of war-time machinery ('first year a drip, second year a trickle, third year a flood'), no fewer than 1,425 cars were then built by high summer 1996. It was at this point, soon after Jaguar's

An early XK8 body shell being built, and carefully checked, for dimensional accuracy.

'shut-down' for the summer break, that what was officially known as '1997 Model Year' assembly began, and the first wave of US-market machines began to fill up the transatlantic 'pipeline'.

The panel on page 141 shows that a small number of 'verification prototypes' had been built towards the end of 1995, and since these took shape when passing down the assembly lines at Browns Lane, the enigma of those statistics makes a lot more sense. Series production did not begin until the last XJS had left the tracks and all manner of changes had been made to the facilities.

There was something of a hiatus at Castle Bromwich, where the bodies were to be built – it was not lengthy, but a definite gap – between the end of old-type XJS assembly, and the start of new-type XK8 assembly. The production, delivery, placing and assembly of major components was always going to be a much more complicated business with the XK8 than it had ever been with the XJS, whose engines – the heart and soul of any car – had been manufactured at Radford, which was just a short distance from Browns Lane, a couple of miles away in another district of Coventry.

Ford's more cosmopolitan approach to purchasing – and its decision to centralize corporate engine production manufacture – meant that the XK8 would take shape in a very different way. It is worth noting that for the very first time since the brand was founded in 1935 (SS-Jaguar) or 1945 (Jaguar), the cars were to be powered by engines that had not been manufactured in Coventry. This was a truly major change, which went almost unnoticed at the time.

In one respect, however, the production of body shells would follow a familiar, even traditional, route. The majority of steel and aluminium pressings, large and small, to make up the complete body shell, would be stamped out at Jaguar's existing Castle Bromwich factory (on the eastern outskirts of Birmingham, and only 15 miles/24km from Browns Lane – the same plant that had always built body shells for the XJS), where they would all then be jigged, welded together and painted. Batches of shells would then be taken to Browns Lane by truck, ready to join the assembly lines alongside the XJ saloons, whose shells had also made an identical journey.

Jaguar made much of the fact that by installing new technology jigging and assembly methods, and by using CAD (computer-aided design) methods to develop the body structure, by comparison with the old XJS they had been able to save quite a lot of weight. According to the official figures, this is how the last of the XJSs compared to the original XK8:

| 1993 XJS (6-litre/V12) | Coupé | 4,101lb |
| | Convertible | 4,377lb |

| 1996 XK8 (4-litre V8) | Coupé | 3,557lb |
| | Convertible | 3,756lb |

In the transition, therefore, from new to old, the weight of the flagship XK had been reduced by 544lb/247kg (Coupé) or 621lb/282kg (Convertible), which was really more than the equivalent of a full family payload and their luggage for a substantial holiday.

Because the XK8 was to use much of the XJS's platform and some inner panels (though there were countless changes and adjustments to be made, and the similarity was by no means complete), volume production could not really begin until the last of the XJS shells had been completed, XJS facilities had been cleared away and the myriad press tool and jigging modifications and modernizations had been made. The new body-in-white assembly line at Castle Bromwich was a complex installation (and expensive – this line alone, well afforested with welding and jigging robots, accounted for one third of total manufacturing investment), and had to settle down – to be 'de-bugged', as it were – before a pre-planned production line speed could be attained.

In the meantime, the multinational business of manufacturing components elsewhere, and then bringing them together, could get under way. As already described, V8 engines were being manufactured at Ford's Bridgend plant in South Wales and trucked to Browns Lane, while five-speed automatic transmissions (ZF) were being made at Friedrichshafen, on the banks of Lake Constance, in Germany, and trucked across Europe for delivery to Browns Lane. Over the years this plant, in fact, had gradually became more of an assembly rather than a manufacturing complex, for little of the

cars was now actually being made there. Trim and woodwork were indeed made on site (Jaguar's 'wood shop' was, rightly, famous for its expertise), but almost everything else was to be brought in from suppliers.

The launch of the new car, at Geneva, was a truly glittering occasion. In an imaginative display, a Coupé was first of all positioned on a turntable, which was all set to revolve throughout the period that the salon was in operation; but on 'press day' the drama leading up to the 'reveal' was heightened because this car was originally covered by a wooden packing case emblazoned with the company's famous 'growler' badge, and the slogan 'Jaguar Cars Ltd, Coventry'. Then, at the final moment, the crate was slowly lifted (by wires slung from the roof of the hall) in a tense, gradual and spine-tingling 'reveal'. As we know, from the scrutiny of Jaguar's own list of verification prototypes, this was actually VP '100', originally assembled in January 1996, then titivated and burnished to a glittering 'show standard' by Jaguar's ultra-experienced Press Office.

With the permission of my old friends at Britain's *Autocar* magazine, this is what they had to say in publishing their show report – editor-in-chief Steve Cropley commented:

This year's show *was* the new Jaguar XK8. As it rotated on the turntable, everyone kept asking everyone else what they thought of it? Controversy centred on four things: space in the wheel arches (too much?), rear body overhang (too great?), over-rider 'teeth' in the nose scoop (too prominent?) and cabin dimensions (too snug?).

At motor shows, new cars have to survive a sort of trial by fire. Hundreds of pundit onlookers dwell endlessly on details artificially highlighted by intense lighting from odd directions. Little of it is relevant to the way the car looks on the road. Russell Bulgin [Steve's colleague] considers the XK8 will be one of the most imposing cars on the road, and I agree. Even on the Geneva rotisserie it looked at least twenty-eight times better than an XJS.

The show report itself was a little more cautious:

So, too, Jaguar's XK8, the starting point of every conversation in the Palais d'Exposition, and probably the most pragmatic example of platform economics. Was it pretty enough? Would it go like it looked? Was it better looking than a DB7? Who cared if it – like the Aston – *was* an XJS?

The new Jaguar, well: what *do* you think? Was it really too curvy? Too airy beneath the wheelarches? Too distant from the carpet? Too retro? Too *Nuevo*? This is how harshly Jaguar's new coupe was assessed. Walking Geneva was to dodge off-the-cuff, off-the-record critiques of the XK8, flying around like so much verbal shrapnel. This is the fundamental dilemma engendered when revealing a new product, heartache made metal, before an audience which, professionally speaking, Knows Too Much.

You find yourself standing alongside a leading car designer as he breaks the XK8 down, element by element – you imagine him mentally CADing the thing into individual pixels – and agreeing that, yes, he's right, the shut-lines are lovely. The shut-lines. Not the power, the torque, the oomph, the go, the stop, the quality, but the cute way those razored filigrees twist and nudge around the lights.

So, naturally, Geneva was vaguely dismissive of the XK8. It couldn't be anything else. That's the way motor shows are: industry ego jammed into a grey double-breasted on an away-day from the executive car park.

What seemed to go without comment – and yet it was a major change from the previous XJS – was that the new XK8 did not have front and rear bumpers: in other words, not separate mouldings or pressings, yet the structure needed to meet USA crash-test legislation, and this was hidden away behind the shapely front and rear parts of the body shell. And then there was the bonnet bulge. Was it even necessary? Functionally, who knows, but for artistic reasons, of course, it was unthinkable that a sporting Jaguar should not have a sleek bulge. The E-Type had had one, the XJS had had one, so why not carry on the tradition?

Cannily, however, Jaguar's publicists wanted two bites at the cherry, for there were no signs of a convertible version of the new car at this time. No secret was made of the imminent arrival of a drop-top version, but Jaguar (and Ford, no doubt) preferred to hold back a few weeks, then to launch that particular type of XK8 at the New York Auto Show in April.

Because this was such an important new model, the motoring media made much of the arrival of the convertible (the car displayed in New York was VP101, which had been prepared alongside VP100 at Whitley in preceding weeks). Jaguar themselves also made much of it, especially by issuing a group picture showing off the XK8 surrounded by classic SS100,

An XK8 Convertible posed in front of several other famous Jaguar roadsters – left to right (at the back) SS100, XK120, E-Type and XJS.

Even if there had been no discreet 'XK8' badge on the tail, in 1996 the shape of this sensational new Jaguar would surely have been recognizable.

When a modern convertible is designed, it is important that the furled soft-top should fold neatly away. This was achieved, beautifully, on the XK8 in 1996.

XK120, E-Type and XJS types. This told such a good story of the way that Jaguar styling had developed over the years, that I have included it on page 73.

As already mentioned above, it emphasized that all previous Jaguar sports cars had had bumpers, but that the XK8 did not – even though those on the E-Type were more for show than for function: on later E-Types in the USA – but not in the UK – the lines of the car were quite ruined by rubber blocks added to help meet the crash test legislation. On the XK8 there were no such protuberances, and the 'over-riders' fixed inside the oval grille were there for visual effect as much as for what they could do to guard against accident damage.

When the New York Show opened its doors in April 1996, it was almost exactly thirty-five years after the E-Type had made its debut in North America. On this occasion, Jaguar chairman Nick Scheele made much of the new car's shape by stating that: 'the dynamic style of the XK8 convertible and coupé can only begin to convey the driving experience in store.' The media couldn't wait – but of course they *had* to wait, for series production had not even begun at that point, so naturally the delivery 'pipeline' from the UK to the USA was still empty.

At the design and development stage, the usual major decisions had had to be made about hood (soft-top) stowage. On the one

Very carefully shot, in the evening sunlight of a Mediterranean harbour location, in 1996 this study showed off the lines of the new XK8, with one of the several optional sets of alloy wheels that were available.

hand, Jaguar still wanted to provide useful, if not ultra-spacious, rear seats, yet to provide adequate headroom in the back. It would have been far too easy to provide a soft top that looked ugly when erect, and over bulky when folded back.

As with the much-admired XJS convertible, which was just about to breathe its last, Fergus Pollock's design team, together with the body engineers, had striven to provide 'coupé refinement' in the convertible itself. Naturally there was not as much cabin space as in the coupé – although there was at least as much as in the XJS, or in those of rivals – but the layout of the retractable top had been finalized without any loss of fuel tank or luggage boot capacities.

The soft top itself was electrically operated, and the frame was double-lined. Not only was there actuation by electric motors from a button in the cabin, but there was automatic latching, and there was also a heated glass rear window. Unlike some other cars in this price bracket, the soft-top did not furl under a movable hard panel, but could be stowed under a soft trim bag.

Mechanically, of course, the convertible was identical with the recently unveiled coupé, which is to say that the 4-litre V8 engine produced 290bhp, a five-speed automatic transmission was standard and so was air conditioning (though the author has often wondered about the expensive wisdom of using air conditioning when the soft-top was furled!). As with the coupé, the convertible featured much wood and leather, all in the usual Jaguar tradition.

It was at this time that Jaguar began to make forecasts about the XK8 production programme. The forecast was that only about 20 per cent of all XK8s built would probably be sold in Britain (this emphasizes, yet again, that without a thriving export market, this sort of British car could never be a viable business proposition), and it was thought that about 40 per cent of those cars would be convertibles.

In 1996, Jaguar made the prediction that, once production built up to its maximum planned rate of 12,000 cars a year, well over half were expected to be sold in North America. In the event, annual production would actually exceed this forecast in three of the next four years. Interestingly enough, it was not until 2002, when the 4.2-litre engine was introduced, that production dropped below the 10,000 per year mark.

When the XK8 was finally launched, Jaguar proudly stated that it could, if pressed, and if everything was going for them, make 368 cars a week, though in practical terms it usually had to settle for no more than, say, 300 to 320 cars. One reason was that much sub-assembly had already been completed before the body shells reached Browns Lane, and another was that the new models were so much easier to build than the old. Jaguar's claim was that although a late-model XJS had taken 138 man hours to be completed, the XK8 required no more than fifty man hours.

Jaguar also made much of the fact that, in their own succinct words, by comparison with the old XJS, the number of separate body panels had been cut by 30 per cent, and the torsional stiffness had been boosted by 25 per cent. Not only that, but the double-wishbone front suspension was all new, as was the speed-sensitive power-assisted steering and the use of multiplex electrical wiring.

This, therefore, was all much more satisfactory than Jaguar had achieved with the old XJS cars since the 1980s. Between 1975 and 1996, XJS annual production had only exceeded 10,000 on two occasions – in 1988 and 1989. By the early 1990s, when X100/XK8 development was well under way, XJS production varied between 3,633 (1992) and 6,918 (1994) cars a year.

In the meantime, and before the first deliveries were made, Jaguar made much of drip-feeding information about the car to the media, in particular with details of the new V8 engine. Market research, they said, had been one major factor in choosing this engine layout (though, as

Trevor Crisp told me, he would have liked it to be just one of three engines – V6, V8 and V12 – in a new strategy). And yes, it really *was* all new, the publicists insisted, for apart from a Woodruff key in the drive line, and the sump plug itself, there was no connection with any other Ford corporate engine, or previous Jaguar power unit.

Having looked carefully at what other manufacturers had on offer – notably the latest state-of-the-art V8s from Lexus (Japanese) and Mercedes-Benz (German) – Jaguar had provided every modern feature. Having tested both, four valves per cylinder were preferred over five per cylinder (three inlet, two exhaust); like Britain's Cosworth race car team (Jaguar talked to them on a regular basis) they never found any power, torque, cost or complexity advantages, and wondered with some puzzlement how a certain rival could have been persuaded otherwise.

The heads themselves featured lines of valves separated by only 28 degrees, cylinder bores were Nicasil-plated, variable inlet camshaft phasing was developed, and a drive-by-wire throttle control was chosen, and nothing other than routine oil and filter changes should be needed for the first 100,000 miles (160,000km). One important feature, which had been taken into account when the design/style was being developed, was that this AJ26 V8 engine was no less than 12in/305mm shorter than the ageing 6-cylinder or V12 types.

First Impressions

When sales actually began in October 1996, one of the most important factors to the new XK8 was not the style, nor the new engine, and not even the 155mph electronically limited top speed – it was the price. When *Autocar* published a four car comparison between the new Jaguar, its kissing cousin the Aston Martin DB7, the BMW 840Ci and the Mercedes-Benz SL500, these current showroom prices tell their own story:

Jaguar XK8 Coupé	**£47,950**
Aston Martin DB7 Coupé	£82,500
BMW 840Ci	£56,850
Mercedes-Benz SL500	£78,950

Jaguar, on the other hand, was still learning fast from Ford (its financial and marketing masters) about the art of offering many, sometimes costly, extras. That same *Autocar* road test car, complete with extras, was price-tagged at £52,285.

Consider, for one moment, that this particular car had CATS (computer-active technology suspension) suspension, along with 18in wheels and fatter tyres, all for £1,350; an upgrade to the sound system – a staggering £1,190; full leather upholstery (£1,415), cruise control (£550) and a CD player for £380. So this was the mid-1990s, and we are not looking back by more than decade – but think how long it would be before cruise control became a standard 'given' on cars of this class and type, and that leather upholstery would be a delete option.

Was it any wonder that, in the summary of its road test, the simple, seven-word conclusion about the Jaguar was 'The best GT in the real world'; and 'It is not unduly dramatic to say the future of Jaguar swivels around the car you see here.' The magazine testers concluded (although you will see that the praise was not all-pervading):

> The XK8 was worth the wait, worth those thousands of miles spent perfecting the ride in America, the sub-zero testing in Lapland, the arguments over its styling that raged for months anywhere from Cologne [Ford-of-Europe's design HQ] to Coventry. It is a truly accomplished GT car, in many ways a more convincing product than the considerably pricier DB7 that proved so influential during its conception and execution.
>
> For starters, it has one of the very best powertrains we've driven at any price. The seamless way in which the five-speed automatic gearbox blends

This was the body assembly line at Castle Bromwich where XK8s took shape in the late 1990s.

with the 4-litre V8 to carry you so immediately, yet so serenely down the road, remains an experience of rare quality, even by today's lofty standards. And the unusually broad vocabulary of the chassis serves only to heighten the respect we harbour for this car on a dynamic level. It is, first and foremost, a cracking good car to drive.

Which is to say nothing of the way it looks, the surprising refinement and economy of its AJ-V8 engine, or the exquisite fit and finish of the body, which features some of the classiest paint, and tightest, most consistent panel gaps of any car. To the outside world, the XK8 is every inch the class act it so richly promises to be.

But beneath that elegant, fluid skin there are glitches, some minor and merely irritating, some not. The fact that there is little or no space in the rear seats for adults is disappointing, but understandable, considering the dreadful interior packaging of the XJS, a car whose basic proportions it was forced to inherit. You either live with this or you don't.

Even in its original form (everyone seemed to know, but would not talk about, the probability of a supercharged derivative joining the range in the future), the XK8 was a very rapid car. Acceleration through the automatic

A proportion of all body shells – this was a convertible – was removed from the end of the Castle Bromwich assembly line, for complete and meticulous dimensional checks.

Jaguar XK8 (Original Model, 1996)

Layout

Unit-construction steel body/chassis structure, 2+2-seater, front engine/rear drive, sold as two-door closed coupé or convertible

Engine

Type	Jaguar AJ-V8
Block material	Cast aluminium
Head material	Cast aluminium
Cylinders	8 in 90-degree V
Cooling	Water
Bore and stroke	86 × 86mm
Capacity	3996cc
Main bearings	5
Valves	4 per cylinder, operated by twin overhead camshafts per cylinder head, with hydraulic phasing of cam timing, and inverted bucket-type tappets
Compression ratio	10.75:1
Fuel supply	Nippondenso fuel injection/engine management system
Max. power	290bhp (DIN) @ 6,100rpm
Max. torque	290lb/ft @ 4,250rpm

Transmission

Manual gearbox not available. Automatic transmission (ZF type) standard

Internal ratios

Top/5th	0.80:1
4th	1.00:1
3rd	1.51:1
2nd	2.20:1
1st	3.57:1
Reverse	4.10:1
Final drive ratio	3.06:1

Suspension and steering

Front	Independent, coil springs, wishbones, anti-roll bar, telescopic dampers
Rear	Independent, double-coil springs, fixed-length drive shafts, lower wishbones, radius arms, twin telescopic dampers
Steering	Rack-and-pinion, power-assisted, 2.8 turns lock to lock
Tyres	245/50ZR-17in, radial ply
Wheels	Cast aluminium disc, bolt-on
Rim width	8in

Brakes

Type	Disc brakes at front and rear, with vacuum servo assistance and anti-lock
Size	12in/305mm diameter front, 12in/305mm diameter rear

Dimensions (in/mm)

Track	Front 59.2/1,504
	Rear 59.0/1,498
Wheelbase	101.9/2,588
Overall length	187.4/4,760
Overall width (incl mirrors)	79.3/2,015
Overall height	
– coupé	51.0/1,296
– cabriolet	51.4/1,306
Unladen weight	Coupé 3,557lb/1,615kg
	Cabriolet 3,756lb/1,705kg

---

transmission (which seemed to exhibit a series of quite seamless ratio changes) was immense, consistent and stirringly effective. With the top speed electronically limited to 155mph/250km/h, this was nevertheless a car that could cruise all day and every day (where it was allowed, of course) at 120mph (190km/h) and more.

Because of the fat tyres, the limited-slip differential, and all the electronic controls in the drive line, little driver's skill was needed to extract the ultimate acceleration: all one had to do was engage 'D', point the car up the road, plant the throttle foot – and watch! 0–60mph took 6.6sec (this was quite a heavy car, don't forget), 0–80mph 10.7sec, 0–100mph in

A proud workforce gathers round the very first completely 'off-tools' XK8, as it drops off the assembly line at Browns Lane in 1996. More than 90,000 would follow in the next decade.

16.7sec, and 0–120mph in 27.1sec. There was quite a lot more to come, of course, and even on German autobahns there was quite a reserve.

All this, of course, came at a price – the price being an overall fuel consumption figure that rarely bettered 20mpg (imperial), though at the fuel prices of the day this was considered quite acceptable, especially as a fuel range of just 400 miles (645km) seemed to be acceptable too. By the cloistered standards of a British motoring writer, this meant that he might leave an English Channel port with a full tank, stop for a refill just once in central France, and reach the Mediterranean without

having to do that again on the same day. And he would, make no mistake, still feel comfortable and quite relaxed at the end of such a journey.

Even at this point, it is worth recalling just how Jaguar had set out to finalize its new model, not least by comparing what they had in mind with the major opposition. Although real-world economics meant that the new car had to take shape around the modified floorplan/platform and suspension layout of the dear old XJS, it needed to be better – not just to look better, but to behave better – than several other competing cars.

81

Testing, testing…does it leak? If it does, find out why, and make sure it doesn't happen again! This was one of Ford's own facilities, of which Jaguar made good use.

Not only did Jaguar find that Pirelli's Italian proving ground was invaluable for developing the right sort of tyres, but there were excellent water-proofing facilities, too.

It was always likely that a new Jaguar would be able to sell at a keener price than anything already on offer from Mercedes-Benz, or any other model from Japan. It was interesting that, at this time, the new Lexus SC400 Coupé from Japan was receiving rave reviews, for its engineering, reliability and build quality – but not for its dynamic qualities. It was because the

Lexus lacked many desirable 'sports car' attributes that Jaguar discarded it from their list of comparator cars.

In addition, although Jaguar respected anything that Porsche might be doing, they did not consider the 911 family as direct competition, which must have been quite a relief to their marketing experts, as that was a rear-engined

Once the designers / stylists had got their hands on the engine bay, much of the detail of the all-new V8 would be hidden away. This, though, was how much testing was done in the early 1990s. Wiring and 'plumbing' too, would be much tidied up before this car reached the showroom.

Oh dear! Can this be serious, or just a colourful mock-up? Let's hope that no private motorist had to find out.

Preparing for 'the reveal' at Geneva in March 1996. The coupé that would be shown to the world's press was under the dust sheet in the foreground, while the mock-up packing case would surround it until the last moment. This was a one-trick wonder, which would only be done once! It had to work – and it did!

XK8 Performance – and its Rivals

Not only was the XK8 a very fast car, but it always offered remarkable value. This simple table shows that the XK8's so-called rivals invariably cost a great deal more to buy. All models except the XKR (which arrived in 1998) were on sale in the UK in 1996/1997.

Car	Maximum speed (mph)	0–60mph (sec)	Standing start ¼-mile (sec)	UK retail price (1997)
XK8	155★	6.6	15.2	£47,950
XKR	157★	5.4	14.0	£59,300 (1998 price)
Aston Martin	157★	5.8	14.3	£78,500 DB7 (6-cyl)
BMW 840 Ci	155★	6.7	n/a	£56,850
Mercedes-Benz SL500	155★	5.9	14.4	£78,950
Porsche 911	173	4.6	13.0	£58,995 Carrera (996 type)

★ Top speed electronically limited

---

masterpiece that seemed to sell in quantities limited only by Porsche's ability to manufacture them in Germany.

When the XK8 was being developed, and when it went on sale, there is no doubt that Jaguar always saw the Mercedes-Benz SL class as its major competition, even though that car was no more of a two-plus-two-seater than was the Jaguar, and even though there was no permanent fixed-head coupé version of the Mercedes model on sale, though a (heavy) lift-off version was available.

The importance of the SL class was not only its versatility (engines between 193bhp/2.8 litres and 394bhp/6 litres were all available, in 6-cylinder, V8 and V12 formats), but that, quite simply, it was a Mercedes. Then, as in most years, cars carrying the three-pointed star badge were looked on as some of the best built cars in the world. There were complaints that prices were high, and that their dealers' attitudes were sometimes snooty, but the build quality of the cars could not usually be faulted.

For the XK8, therefore, Jaguar had set out to build the cars to a standard never previously approached, especially at Browns Lane, where the assembly lines and the construction methods were still being dragged up to contemporary standards by Ford. It was noticeable that they were not willing to deliver cars in the UK until the last months of 1996, nor to begin selling cars in the USA until 1997, if only so they could cram in a few more final improvements and refinements beforehand.

Once they went on sale, the public, like the media, greeted the new XK8 models warmly. It was not that the last of the XJSs had been bad cars – the final cars were, in all fairness, the best of a long pedigree, and were still selling strongly – but they were old designs. As with so many other cars that lived for many years, the clientèle eventually tired of the same looks and the same character.

Published below, this very simple list of production achievements shows just how the XK8 rejuvenated Jaguar's sporty car line, and

Yes, there really is a prototype XK8 under all that disguise. Not even the most diligent spy photographer, though, could identify the car that was hidden away. This was 1993, and the actual chassis was MP19 – where MP stands for 'mechanical prototype'.

brought a smile back to the faces of dealer salesmen all over the world:

Year	Model	Production
1992	XJS	3,633
1993	XJS	5,192
1994	XJS	6,918
1995	XJS	4,884
1996	XJS	1,608
- - - - - - - -		
1996	XK8	7,112
1997	XK8 and XKR	14,929
1998	XK8 and XKR	13,221
1999	XK8 and XKR	11,421
2000	XK8 and XKR	12,241

In other words, by comparing the last full year of XJS production (1995) with the first full year of XK8 (1997), it is clear that demand had leapt by 300 per cent. Agreed, the XK8 was benefiting from the 'halo effect' that surrounds most new models, but this was a remarkable boost. Although I do not know what rate of sales were needed for the company to call the new XK8 a profitable venture, this must have been a very encouraging trend.

What made the XK8 such a promising new arrival was that it was, literally, new. No longer would Jaguar sales staff have to make excuses for the sporty two-plus-two seaters they were anxious to sell; no longer would they have to make excuses for styling that had not really changed for twenty years. On the other hand, the truly engineering-savvy among them could make it clear that most of the engineering was brand new, but that some of the very best chassis features of the old XJS were being continued.

For the time being, however, there was only one apparently retrograde step to be explained away. The last of the XJSs had boasted a 308bhp/6-litre/V12 engine, whereas the first of the XK8s 'only' had a 290bhp/4-litre/V8 power unit. The public found it easier to compare figures like that, than to be convinced that the new car actually had a better power/weight ratio than before – 183bhp/ton for the original XK8, compared with 168bhp/ton for the last of the XJSs. Also, the fact that the XK8 was a more fuel-efficient car than its ancestor was often ignored.

In the end, though, none of this mattered as much as it might have done with a more ordinary car, for the XK8 was the sort of machine that flattered one's senses. Not only was it a very fast machine – any car that could leap up to 100mph (160km/h) in little more than 15sec was going to qualify for that exclusive category – but it achieved everything in such an effortless way. Never, for one moment, did the engine feel as if it were working hard,

never did the automatic transmission feel as if it were being stressed, and never did the driver feel that he was having to try at all hard to extract the most from the XK8. Show it a horizon, and the XK8 would leap towards it, show it any road that was less than smooth, and it would seem to iron out the imperfections – it all seemed to effortless, so dignified, and so capable.

So, was the style just millimetres less than totally exquisite? Was the performance just less than sensational? And was the XK8 just ever-so-slightly less than exclusive? Maybe it was – but it was also something better than all of its distinguished rivals. It was also much, much cheaper, and didn't show it.

So what if an all-new XK8 was marginally slower than the closely related Aston Martin DB7 – which, by the way, had a technologically old straight 6-cylinder engine? Some would say that it looked just as wonderfully sinuous – and it was £35,550 cheaper. And how much was that in the world of 1996? That was enough to pay for a Land Rover Discovery as a truly up-to-date go-anywhere 4×4 model, along with a Ford Ka for use as the family runabout. And wasn't this all proof that, although Jaguar's founder Sir William Lyons was now dead and gone, his cost-containing spirit lived on?

5 XKR – Supercar Performance

By 1998, the more excitable motoring enthusiasts' magazines could barely contain themselves. Right from the start, they had gathered that a supercharged version of the new V8 engine would eventually be added to the XK8 range, that this car would be called XKR (earlier there was a supercharged version of the XJ8 saloon called the XJR, so this made logical sense), and the prospects were quite mouth-watering. If the 290bhp XK8

Compare the styling differences between the XK8 and this high-performance derivative, the original XKR of the late 1990s. The XKR, of course, featured a supercharged V8 engine, cooling louvres in the bonnet panel, and a different front grille with mesh as a styling motif.

With all that power hidden away behind the front of a supercharged Jaguar like the XKR Silverstone, a large front grille was needed to channel all the cooling air into the engine bay.

Because the XK8/XKR was based on the platform of the XJS model, some testers found that the space in the cabin was somewhat restricted. Although four seats were provided (this is an XKR), the rears were strictly 'occasional', and were not really usable by adults.

Just like the old days! Coachbuilders always liked to identify 'their' bodies by plates on the door sills – which is precisely how Jaguar identified the XKR Silverstone in 2000.

This discreet little badge on the glove box was one of the few ways in which Jaguar identified the 'Silverstone' limited edition.

Supercharged XKR models used a Mercedes-Benz five-speed automatic transmission, but were fitted with the familiar type of 'J-gate' selector lever in the centre console.

could reach 155mph (250km/h) and have some of its ultimate top-end performance cut off by electronic means, then how much power would be available (or needed) in the XKR, and just how fast would it be? The fact that some of Europe's car manufacturers (notably not the Italian supercar makers) agreed among themselves that 155mph (250km/h) was enough for a modern sporting car, meant that none of them had any need to search for the last few horsepower that might, just might, be available.

Although Jaguar's engineers, naturally, would have liked to make the forthcoming new XKR even more different and even faster than it eventually was – and, believe me, they had all the toys in the locker, and all the prototype experience, to make it so – there were, of course, cost constraints to add to the limited top-speed political constraints, too. Ford, their masters, and that all-powerful corporate function within the empire called 'product planning', thought they knew just

how far they could go without driving up costs (and therefore the selling price) completely out of sight.

Because of Jaguar's sheer shortage of resources at this time – tight constraints on space at Whitley, on capital available and, equally important, on key engineers – very little of the work that would go into finalizing the XKR could be done while the XK8 itself was still on the secret list. Engine work, of course, had been going ahead for some time, as had an investigation into automatic transmission supplies, but little more.

The result, after a lot of planning, testing and development, was that the launch of the XKR had to be delayed until March 1998. This was when we saw an important derivative of the XK8 that had very few styling changes – the cooling louvres in the bonnet panel, and different wheels were obvious recognition points – but this was balanced by a great deal of extra performance, and by a long list of detail engineering changes under the skin.

'Blowing' the Engine

As project chief Bob Dover and engine expert Trevor Crisp both told me on separate occasions, if Jaguar were to provide an XK8-based car with 350–400bhp, it would have to be done with a forced induction engine. For many reasons, some fundamental, some detail, the use of a supercharger always looked more promising than that of a turbocharger. In fact, once Jaguar opted for the supercharger solution, it remained faithful to it for many years to follow. And for why? Rolls-Royce/Bentley, after all, had made a different choice, which was to turbocharge their venerable V8, while Ford's Cosworth subsidiary had been hired to turbocharge the modern BMW V8 for use in the still-secret Bentley Arnage.

The problem, as Jaguar saw it, was a combination of packaging, of cost, and of meeting forthcoming regulations, and the sort of power envisaged as necessary for an XKR could not be found with a normally aspirated tune-up. The new, normally aspirated AJ-V8 4-litre V8 was good for 290bhp, all delivered with great dignity and flexibility, but there wasn't much more in reserve without applying the sort of tuning expertise that would make that excellent engine less flexible, more noisy, and certain to produce more exhaust emissions. Furthermore, Jaguar never even considered reverting to an XJS-derived power unit because, now unable to meet a raft of modern legislative requirements, the last of the mighty 6-litre V12s had been put under sentence of death (the last was to be produced in 1997): it was heavy, and costly, too.

Was there any other possibility in the locker? Only the still-developing new-generation V12 that Cosworth was productionizing for Ford, and which was about to be offered in the Aston Martin DB7. This had started life, effectively, as two American-designed 3-litre V6s joined end to end (not actually, of course, but the visual analogy was clear), but it had changed a lot along the way. Functionally, that would have been a great power unit, and building such a 6-litre with a completely reliable 400bhp would have been no problem at all for Cosworth – in fact it would initially be rated at 420bhp for the DB7 Vantage – and there was no doubt that it could be fitted into the existing engine bay of the XK8. There was, however, one big snag at this time: Ford and Cosworth were only planning to lay down enough production capacity – machining, assembly and testing – at Cosworth's Wellingborough factory for it to be built at a rate of hundreds – not thousands – every year. So even though Jaguar's initial estimate of XKR sales was only 500 cars a year (though happily they were soon proved to be wrong, for actual demand soared far above that), that extra requirement would completely swamp Wellingborough. So here was another engine that was likely to cost too much to build.

Well before design work on the original X100/XK8 model had been completed, therefore, project work had begun on a 'blown' version of the brand-new AJ-V8 engine. From the very start, Jaguar's 'packaging' engineers made sure that an AJ-V8, complete with all the extra 'add-ons' that forced induction would require, could easily be fitted.

The big decision, which virtually none of the pundits (uninformed engineers, outside the company) had been expecting, was that the 'blown' power unit would be a supercharged engine (the magic word in all this, which I will shortly explain, being 'Eaton') rather than a turbocharged engine. This was a real surprise, as in most other recent cases where a choice had had to be made, certainly in the last two decades, other companies had opted for turbocharging rather than supercharging.

In engineering terms, superchargers and turbochargers both help to boost the power of an engine by pushing more fuel/air mixture through the inlet manifolding into the cylinders, thereby effectively increasing the size, and therefore the potential power output, of an engine, but they do it in different ways.

Turbochargers – which look like miniature gas turbine engines in some ways – use centrifugal blowers to boost inlet gas pressure, and are driven by gas turbines, which are them-selves driven by waste exhaust gases as they leave the engine. Superchargers, on the other hand, are really mechanical pumps of one or other rotary types, which are driven from an engine's crankshaft by belts, chains or a gear-ing system.

Each system has advantages, each one disad-vantages. Because a turbocharger operates as a 'free spirit', being impelled by hot exhaust gases that would otherwise go to waste out of the exhaust pipes, it provides power for free, but for gas-flow reasons rarely starts to work at all efficiently until the engine is spinning at 2,500rpm or more. On the other hand, because it is linked directly to the engine by physical means (by gearing, or by a belt drive), a supercharger starts to provide a boosted charge from very low rpm, though ultimately perhaps not quite as much at the top end: the down side is that quite a lot of horsepower has to be used up to drive it.

Earlier in the 1990s, Jaguar did much testing, concluding that each system had certain advan-tages in certain applications. Because turbo engines tended to work best by providing peak torque, and peak efficiency, higher up the rev range, they suit sporty cars better than they suit saloons. Jaguar, though, wanted to produce a 'blown' engine that would be suitable for use in the XK8 and also in the XJ8 saloon where, in each case, a seamless surge of extra power could be more valuable and more suitable.

And so it was that the supercharged solution was finally chosen. The instrument chosen to deliver the extra power was an M112 Eaton supercharger, a Roots-type component with interlinked vanes. This bulky but nevertheless slim item fitted neatly inside the top of the cylinder block V itself. Unlike a turbocharger, this supercharger was not about sudden surges of torque, or about the spluttering and chat-tering of a wastegate when the driver lifted his right foot – though not even Jaguar had been able to eliminate the urgent and spine-tingling wail that gradually swelled as the engine revs rose, merely attenuate it.

Although the nominal compression ratio had been reduced to a mere 9:1 (the normal-ly aspirated engine's ratio was 10.75:1, of course), it all helped to produce a real surge of extra power. This is the comparison between the two engines in 1998 form:

Peak power	*Peak torque*
(bhp/rpm)	*(lb.ft/rpm)*
XK8 (normally aspirated)	
290bhp/6,100rpm	290lb.ft/4,250rpm
XKR (supercharged)	
370bhp/6,150rpm	387lb.ft/3,600rpm

Therefore not only had supercharging added 80bhp and nearly 100lb.ft of torque, but the torque peak had been clawed back by 650rpm, and the new engine was astonishingly flexible.

Jaguar, Eaton and Superchargers

Although Jaguar eventually chose Eaton – a com-pany based in Cleveland, USA – to supply super-chargers for its AJ-V8 engine, this company was already well known to other constituents of the Ford empire. Eaton had been producing blowers for some years, particularly for North American automotive and aerospace concerns, and was well known and well respected by Ford-USA before it did its first business with Jaguar.

Ford-Europe has reminded me that although the basic Roots supercharger technology dates back to the early twentieth century, Eaton first supplied automotive superchargers for Ford's pri-vate car development departments in the 1980s. For private car usage, the first-generation Eaton supercharger was originally fitted to the overhead-valve 3.8-litre V6 engine installed in the Ford-USA Thunderbird Super Coupé of 1989: at this point it was rated at 213bhp (nett), and was set to provide boost up to 0.8 bar.

The third-generation Eaton/Roots blower was then fitted to the Aston Martin DB7, but it was a larger version of this design that was later stan-dardized on the XKR and other Jaguar models of the late 1990s.

ABOVE: *As if you needed a reminder…. This XKR badge indicated that, compared with less specialized XK8s, the XKR had an extra 80bhp and even more performance.*

LEFT: *In 2000, XKR SVO and XKR Silverstone models were easily identified by these massive 20in diameter BBS alloy wheels, and the Jaguar-badged Brembo brake callipers.*

No extravagant spoilers, no extrovert badging, no unique paint jobs – the XKR looked almost exactly like the original XK8, but was even faster.

No, the XKR Silverstone did not have an image of the Jaguar R1 F1 car on the bonnet – this was merely an artist's mock-up for the launch. The 'Silverstone' badge was real, though.

This was the discreet new badge which was worn by all limited-edition 'Silverstone' models, there being an 'XKR' badge on the tail.

The overall effect, therefore, was of a much broader-shouldered engine that delivered 28 per cent more peak power and no less than 33 per cent extra peak torque, always in a smooth and totally effortless manner.

Even so, no more than minor changes had been needed to accommodate this engine. After opening up the bonnet panel, the neat way in which the Eaton supercharger was packaged was obvious, but Jaguar had not needed to make more than minor changes to the exhaust system, the engine calibration and the cooling arrangements. Here was a colossally powerful engine that still idled sweetly, and without temperament: nor was it one that pushed masses of surplus hot air back towards the cabin.

Much hardware was squeezed into the independent rear suspension region of the XKR – here fitted with the rarely seen 20in BBS alloy wheels, and the cross-drilled Brembo disc brakes and rotors.

The Roots-type Eaton supercharger fitted to XKRs was neatly packaged, mounted on top of the cylinder block and belt-driven from the nose of the crankshaft.

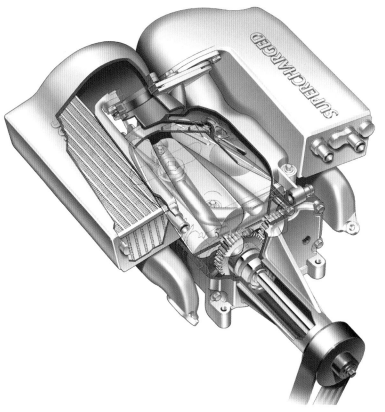

Automatic Transmission – by Courtesy of Mercedes-Benz

Intriguingly, when Jaguar came to develop the XKR (and the XJR saloon with which it would have to share so much), the engineers rapidly concluded that the XK8's newly finalized five-speed ZF automatic transmission would not be up to dealing with the extra torque of the supercharged engine. ZF, naturally, were mortified to know this, especially as they had no alternative heavier-duty automatic transmission to offer in its place immediately – but they could, at least, use their good offices in Germany to fill the gap. But when Jaguar researched the market place to find a suitable automatic transmission to use with the massive torque of the new supercharged engine – especially as they knew, though the average Jaguar enthusiast did not, that a larger-capacity and even more powerful V8 would be launched in the next few years – they rapidly concluded that there were few readily available transmissions that might be suitable.

Jaguar's needs were very demanding. The company wanted to use a box with five forward ratios, and one that was 'politically' available – in other words, from a company, independent or otherwise, which would not object to doing business with a Ford-controlled organization. In previous periods, Jaguar-without-Ford could have spread its net more widely, but not any more. In North America this almost automatically ruled out using anything from General Motors or the Chrysler Corporation, and there was nothing remotely matching their requirements outside Europe. From Ford-USA, Lincoln's automatics were four-speeders, and Ford itself could not offer anything with the required torque capacity.

Jaguar therefore had to make a trawl around Europe, and soon concluded that there was only one likely candidate – from Mercedes-Benz! Interestingly, Porsche had recently been through the same analytical process, and reached the same conclusions. The unpalatable fact was that the Stuttgart-based Mercedes-Benz concern, whose products could definitely be seen as direct competition for Jaguar, had an own-brand five-speed automatic transmission, which they were currently matching to their own 6-litre/394bhp V12 engine (as used in the S600 and the SL600 models).

But would Mercedes-Benz want to do business with Jaguar, when the forthcoming XJR and XKR types looked like being head-on competition for both these German products, and why should they bother? Happily for all concerned, Mercedes-Benz decided to do the deal, and were ready to supply Jaguar by the autumn of 1997. This was a very civilized arrangement, because their refusal would have killed off the XJR/XKR models at that time, and reduced the competition that Mercedes-Benz had to face.

Chassis

Fortunately, Jaguar already knew what had to be done to make the XK8 'chassis' – including the front and rear suspension, brakes and steering installations – cope with the extra power and torque of the XKR, and if the truth were told, they realized that the braking system was perhaps not quite up to the job of keeping 370bhp in check.

Visually, little had changed around the chassis, though spring and damper settings had been revised. The Servotronic power-assisted steering had been revisited and revised – such that the distinguished classic car writer Mark Hughes later commented that:

> The result is brilliant. Fingertip control remains around town, but messages beneath the lightness are so clear that merely turning through junctions is enjoyably tactile. Gradual weight build-up with speed, however, is sufficiently marked to endow a genuine sporting edge. There's now enough tension behind steering-wheel movement to make the XKR a car you grab hold of, and hustle through corners with your wrists.

Jaguar XKR (Original 1998 Type)

Specification as for XK8 of the period, except for:

Engine

Compression ratio	9.0:1
Fuel supply	Nippondenso fuel injection/engine management system, with Eaton supercharger, maximum boost 0.8bar
Max. power	376bhp (DIN) @ 6,150rpm
Max. torque	387lb.ft @ 3,600rpm

Transmission

	Manual gearbox not available. Automatic transmission (Mercedes-Benz type) standard

Internal ratios

Top/5th	0.83
4th	1.00
3rd	1.41
2nd	2.19
1st	3.59:1
Reverse	3.15:1
Final drive ratio	3.06:1

Suspension and steering

Tyres	(F) 245/45ZR–18in, (R) 255/45ZR–18in, radial ply
Wheels	Cast aluminium disc, bolt-on
Rim width	(F) 8in, (R) 9in

Brakes

Type	Disc brakes at front and rear, with vacuum servo assistance and anti-lock
Size	12.8in/325mm diameter front, 12in/305mm diameter rear

Dimensions

Unladen weight	Coupé 3,616lb/1,640kg Cabriolet 3,859lb/1,750kg

The other important advance is that a new development, 'computer active technology suspension' (in view of the make of this car, the CATS acronym was singularly apt!), was standardized, and became optional on the normally aspirated XK8. This was done by providing electronically controlled adaptive damping, which, allied to the firmed-up springing, made this a heavy car that really could be tossed about at will. Power oversteer (of course – what else did you expect from a 370bhp car!) was easy to provoke, but equally easy to control.

It helped, of course, that 18in Pirelli P Zero tyres had been standardized – the author owned a car with P Zeros and can vouch for them – with 8in wide front rims, and no less than 9in wide rear rims.

Style

Because the XKR arrived so closely after the launch of the original XK8 – just eighteen action-filled months, during which the first 20,000 XK8s had already been built – Jaguar had neither the excuse, nor the ability, to make any serious style (what modern engineers would call 'design') changes.

The overall style – all sweeping curves, proportions and sinuous aerodynamically efficient features – was not changed. Enthusiasts, however, could easily identify the XKR from the XK8, not only by the functional cooling louvres in the bonnet panel (there were two blocks – one on each side of the central bulge), but by a different grille, different alloy wheels, and of course by the badges themselves. At the front, in particular, the head-on Jaguar 'grinner' was still in pride of place, but the wording around it stated 'JAGUAR SUPERCHARGED', which made a most emphatic point.

Although it was still the same size and oval shape as before – there were no sheet metal changes to the panels surrounding it – the grille now featured a simple mesh, and we were assured that this channelled more fresh air into the engine bay than before. Twin 'overriders', quite useless because of the way in which they were positioned within that oval, were retained. At the rear, too, a discreet transverse spoiler on the tail made slight differences both to the looks and to the aerodynamic performance of the car itself.

Incidentally, some said that the louvres in the bonnet panel were not entirely functional, but were there partly because they might remind everyone of another classic Jaguar that had a louvred bonnet − the E-Type. Jaguar insist that the louvres were purely functional, and that the engine would overheat if they were not included.

Astonishing Performance

Enthusiasts needed little training to realize that the new supercharged engine had transformed the performance of Jaguar's latest sporty machine. Not only were the benefits of the 28 per cent extra power very obvious, but the faster you drove, the more obvious they became. Except for the XJ220 supercar − a limited-production machine that surely doesn't count, in the same way that the XKSS of the late 1950s would not have counted either − the new XK8 was the most quickly accelerating Jaguar ever built up to this time.

Performance figures by comparison with rivals are published in the panel on page 86, but it is worth noting that the XKR was more than one second faster over the standing ¼-mile sprint, which, considering the weight of the machine, was quite remarkable. When indulging in flat-out driving, of course, it was best not to think of the limited life of the rather soft compound P-Zero tyres.

Jaguar made much of one statistic, which I am sure was carefully chosen to raise a few eyebrows: it claimed that the standard XKR would accelerate up to its artificially limited top speed of 155mph (250km/h) in 39.3sec, whereas the XK8 would take 105.6sec! However, one wonders how much of that minute-long delay by the XK8 was caused by it

crawling up to the last two or three mph, for the performance difference was surely not that stark?

Yet the fact was, that an unfettered XKR could certainly reach 175mph (280km/h), and maybe more, which put it on a par with previous, expensive and relatively uncivilized cars such as the Ferrari 365GTB4 Daytona. So could it be the fastest ever, front-engined car? Maybe it was, and maybe it wasn't − but certainly, no other car could achieve what it did, without any semblance of fuss or temperament. By courtesy of *Autocar*, here is a simple flat-out acceleration contrast between the two types:

Acceleration (secs)	XK8 (1996)	XKR (1998)
0–30mph	2.3	2.2
0–40mph	3.4	3.1
0–50mph	4.9	4.2
0–60mph	6.6	5.4
0–70mph	8.4	6.9
0–80mph	10.7	8.9
0–90mph	13.5	11.0
0–100mph	16.7	13.3
Standing start ¼-mile	15.2	14.0

On the Market

No sooner was the XKR put on sale than it began to confound the forecasts made for it by Jaguar's marketing staffs. In the beginning, they say, Jaguar had expected only a 5 per cent boost from the arrival of the XKR, but in its first year (1978) no fewer than 17 per cent of sales went to the supercharged car, while 30 per cent of 1999 sales were of XKRs.

Helped along by its great success in the XJR saloons, this supercharged engine made a great impact on the market place, for it was selling in a market sector where customers thought little of fuel costs, and were equally as concerned with the performance of their new car compared with that of its rivals. This was, for

Emphasizing yet again Jaguar's long-term connection with the Silverstone race track, this posed shot, at Woodcote corner, shows an XKR Silverstone, with the high-speed fire-tender used in the early stages of every race at this circuit.

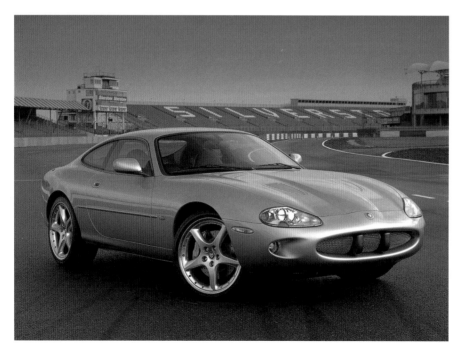

Why spend so much more money on an Aston Martin or on a foreign car, when you could have an XK8 Silverstone instead?

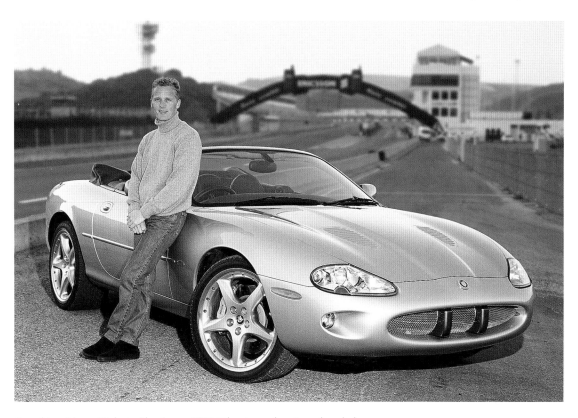

Race driver Johnny Herbert with a Jaguar XKR Silverstone, when it was launched.

The interior of the XKR family was much more 'gentlemen's club' than 'trendy whizz-bang', with real leather seating, and real wood on the facia/ instrument panel.

Depending on what colour was chosen, the bonnet louvres of the XKR were almost hidden away.

BBS wheels like this – gold on the SVO and silver on the 'Silverstone' – were even wider and more effective than the standard items.

XKR types fitted with the supercharged 370bhp engine needed a lot of cooling air to be guided through the front intake, which explains the use of a grille mesh.

sure, not a car about which any motoring enthusiast could remain indifferent for long. Even Britain's *Car* magazine, noted for its dyspeptic view of most British supercar engineering, was in awe of the XKR's abilities. As John Simister wrote, in the course of a multi-car comparison test:

> The steering is quick, accurate, and as free of rubbery interplay as any Jaguar's has yet been, yet the suspension is actually better at soaking up bumps than the normal XK8's. The effect is of a smaller,

wieldier XJR – which, mechanically, the XKR is. All XK8s should feel like this. As the changes are to be applied across the range, future ones will.

There are some aspects of the XKR that aren't so great, though. The view over your shoulder is hopeless, sacrificed to thick pillars and a rising waistline, so parking is an act of faith. The great plank of dashboard in wood is too much of a good thing to some eyes, though I quite like it.

And the key fob brushes my right knee, as it does in all Jaguars. But as I floor the drive-by-wire throttle at 100mph, hear a super-slidy-synchronous down-shift into third gear and hurtle towards our 13.1mpg test fuel consumption result, I can overlook these little imperfections. This newest Jaguar is a rollicking good drive.

All very well, but the conclusion of this visually spectacular feature surprised everyone. Seven supercars had attended the same wet and gloomy spring day in the mountain of Wales; after several other cars had been dismissed:

It falls, then, to the 911 [Porsche 911 Carrera] and the XKR, and deciding between them is mighty difficult. The Porsche is more physical, so your drive will be more exciting. The Jaguar handles the drama for you, so your drive will be more relax-

ing. Both are massively quick, on straight roads and through corners, and neither intimidates its driver. That the Jaguar is an automatic might trouble a keen driver, but it shouldn't because it's such a willing drive partner.

Deep breath, and final weighing up. The Jaguar's monstrous, relentless torque is wholly addictive and completely thrilling, but you can arrive at your destination unshaken, even though you have been stirred. Pace is mixed with true civility and a remarkable ride. It wins.

This was undoubtedly a remarkable conclusion, and it is not exaggerating to say that Jaguar was really quite stunned by it, especially as the Porsche 911 was such an icon then.

The XK8 Silverstone meant business, in any conditions and any temperatures.

How many XK8s were ever driven to the limit of their capabilities? Not many, if the surveys are accurate – but the supercharged variety were certainly among the world's fastest cars in the early 2000s.

Although the XKR Silverstone was a big, heavy car, it was still at home at high speed on a race track.

The five-spoke wheels on the Silverstone certainly meant business, and simply enormous brakes were needed to keep all that performance in check.

At the time, *Car* magazine was one of those read and absorbed by everyone, even if some did not like to admit it (perhaps like a written version of the *Top Gear* TV programme), so this verdict must have been just one of the factors that added to demand in the next few years. Another, no doubt, was that in that seven car comparison it became clear that the XKR cost £59,975 when the 911 Carrera cost £64,650.

XKR SVO

Ford, in the meantime, had been pressing ahead in its attempt to squeeze more and more sales out of Jaguar. By looking at what had already succeeded with its own brand, it concluded that a special department, building special versions of its cars, might also be successful – the result being the launch of Jaguar SVO (which

meant 'Special Vehicle Operations') in 1999. Something like this had been done once before, when the still-independent Jaguar had got together with Tom Walkinshaw's TWR organization to set up JaguarSport. Not only had a series of faster, more specialized XJ-S cars been sold, but that operation had also developed and built the commercially unsuccessful XJ220 supercar. But that was then and this was the late 1990s: Walkinshaw's links with Jaguar had long since been severed, but Jaguar decided to try again.

The first evidence of this philosophy came with the showcasing of SVO components on the prototype XK180 Roadster, but there was a commercially important showing at the Frankfurt Motor Show in September 1999. It was here that a range of components (there was no fixed specification kit) was shown on saloons and on the XK8; called R Performance, it brakes (not only impressively large, at 13.2in/335mm at the front, and 13.0in/330mm at the rear, but ventilated and cross-drilled for maximum cooling effect), along with uprated springs and stiffer front and rear anti-roll bars, as well as retuned, variable ratio power-assisted steering. The ride height was reduced by 0.4in/10mm.

When it tested a car in October 1999, *Autocar* magazine, while being distinctly sniffy about the original XKR – 'In truth, the XKR's brakes, handling and steering invariably fell apart if the car was really stretched over a challenging road' – was much happier about the R Performance/SVO package, even if it did cost an extra £5,900, bringing up the cost of the complete car to £66,055. Even so:

> Larger brakes need large wheels to hide behind, and the new XKR's wheel options don't disappoint. It's a staggering reflection on the advances in technology that the 20in diameter BBS alloys fitted here are as wide as an original Mini wheels were tall. Ten inches, to be precise, with nine-inch items at the front. The SVO's Pirelli P-Zero tyres are also vast…until now this sort of rubber has been the standard fare of German tuning companies, but not traditional British sports car makers.
>
> Huge rubber was always going to have a detrimental effect on ride quality, but the differences over the standard car are actually surprisingly marginal. There are rumbles over poor surfaces and a greater tendency to 'tramline' under heavy braking. Stiffer springs and low-profile tyres don't help the low-speed ride either, but the payback comes as speeds rise. The body control is noticeably tauter and sharper than before, the SVO Jag retaining its damping composure at speed long after the standard car has started to crumble.
>
> By sending it to the fettlers at SVO, Jaguar has come close to turning a good car into a great one, for in many ways all that stood between the XKR and pure genius was a decent braking system. For us, however, the lack of proper feel to the steering still prevents it from crossing that increasingly thin line that separates inspired supercars from merely very capable fast coupés.

Special Vehicle Operations

Until Ford stabilized Jaguar's finances, it could not encourage too much off-the-wall enterprise among its engineers. By the early 1990s, however, it was clear that a self-starting team should be set up to tackle the special jobs for which Jaguar was always being approached. Soon after the old Daimler DS420 Limousine had gone out of production at Browns Lane (where assembly had latterly taken place in a dedicated closed-door part of the complex), the remnants of this operation were named Special Vehicle Operations (SVO – Ford always loved acronyms), and started building specials such as cars for the British royal family, other VIPs and the police, plus race-track fire tenders, and cars such as the Daimler Corsica show car. Where necessary (especially in design terms) they could call in expertise from other departments. As the then chairman, Nick Scheele, commented in 1998:

> The XK180 graphically illustrates the skills we have available in SVO. While most customers are satisfied with the specification and performance of their cars, a number have asked for a more individual approach. SVO will be able to satisfy this demand.

It was because of these abilities that SVO, rather than Jaguar's mainstream engineering operation, tackled the development and building of the two XK180 project cars.

included new chassis equipment, but no changes to engine tune.

Among the newly launched items were 18in, or even 20in diameter BBS aluminium road wheels, huge ventilated disc brakes, and firmer, more responsive sports suspensions. On the XK8 and XKR8, what were branded as 'Milan' road wheels were offered for £1,950, or if the owner didn't consider that was quite enough, he could specify differently styled 20in wheels and ultra-low-profile tyres (255/35 section at the front, 285/30 at the rear) for £2,950.

The optional handling pack included the larger wheels, the newly finalized Brembo

XKR Silverstone

Even so, it was only months before Jaguar pushed the margins of XKR performance and behaviour even further, for in April 1990 it showed off another special edition – the XKR Silverstone. The difference between this car and other limited-edition Jaguars, is that it was the very first to be approved by the new owner, Ford. To Uncle Henry, special-edition machinery was something their sales and marketing staff could evolve at the drop of a hat, but for Jaguar it was quite novel.

The excuse – and all marketing people need an excuse for this sort of thing – was that Jaguar had just entered the high-octane world of Formula One, so they decided to link Silverstone, which is usually claimed as the home of British motor racing, with the XKR. The result was a car that took the entire XKR theme one stage further onwards, and upwards – for which the British buyer was asked to pay £66,785 (Coupé) or £72,185 (Convertible). In fact it was *very* strictly 'limited edition', for only fifty such Coupés and fifty Convertibles were built.

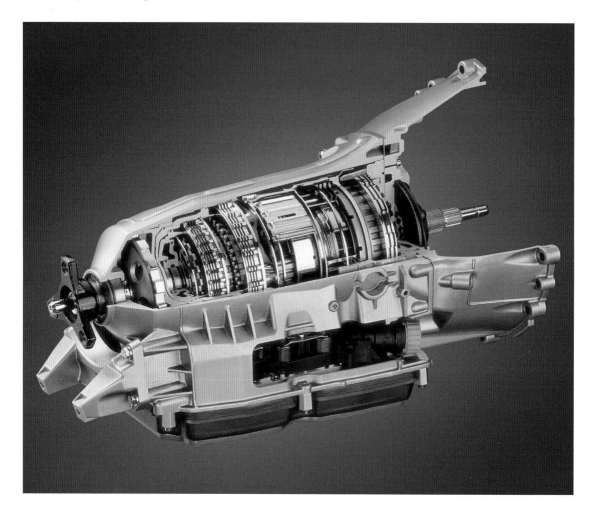

This was the display assembly of the Mercedes-Benz five-speed automatic transmission chosen by Jaguar to mate with the supercharged 370bhp engine of the XKR. There isn't a millimetre of wasted space in there.

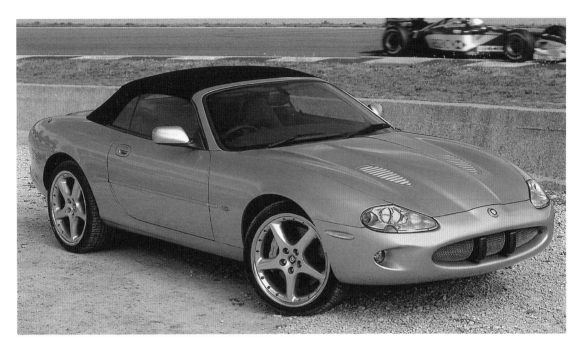

Carefully posed to signal the connection between road- and race-car Jaguars, the XKR Silverstone is being passed by the Jaguar R1 Formula One car of 2000.

Considering that this transmission was intended to deal with the massive power torque of the Jaguar XKR, this Mercedes-Benz five-speed automatic transmission was a compact miracle.

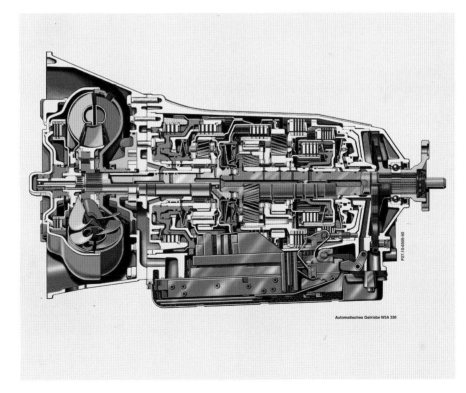

What a wonderfully atmospheric shot, as produced by Jaguar-USA's publicists in 1996. What better way could there be of showing how that indefinable Jaguar 'something' had filtered down over the years? Going progressively back from the cameras lens is an early XK8, an XJS, an E-Type, an XK120 and an SS100. All of them desirable and, collectively, worth a king's ransom.

Mechanically, and in its style, the Silver-stone was a direct development of the XKR SVO, with effectively the same chassis and 370bhp running gear, but with even more attention to detail style and decoration. Every single one of the Jaguar 'R' performance options was fitted as standard, including the latest type of 20in BBS alloy wheels, the huge Brembo disc brakes (355mm front, 330mm rear, cross-drilled disc rotors and all), the firmed-up suspension and anti-roll bars, and (in this special case) a chance to spend a day with the F1 team at Silverstone for the British GP in 2000.

Jaguar in Formula 1

Although not a single item in the Jaguar F1 cars of 2000–2004 was Jaguar based (the use of the 'Jaguar' name was mere-ly a Ford rebranding exercise on cars that had already been engineered by Jackie Stewart's team), the company tried its best to reap any positive publicity from what became rather a lacklustre programme. To produce a 'Jaguar' F1 team, Ford bought out the Stewart F1 operation, retained the Cosworth V10 engines that had latterly powered those cars (Ford also owned Cosworth Racing at this time), and progressively modernized the ex-Stewart factory at Milton Keynes.

Except in terms of the publicity and public affairs activities surrounding the F1 team, Jaguar F1 and Jaguar the road car company were totally separated. However, to help launch the F1 team, and to link Jaguar road cars more closely with British motor racing, the 'Silverstone' badge was chosen for the special edition XKR introduced in April 2000.

Did you know that Jaguar's phenomenal supercharged AJ8 engine also found a home in four-wheel-drive Range Rovers in the early 2000s? This was the Range Rover Sport application.

SVO Cars – More Tweaks for 2001

Four months later, with the 100-off XKR Silverstones all made, and sold, Jaguar upgraded the basic design yet again. Calling it nothing more than XKR 2001, the team phased in a car that was still no faster (though wasn't 370bhp quite enough for everyone?), but had more safety and technical features than ever before.

The latest type of tail lamps – a feature shared with other XKs, for obvious series production reasons – had what Jaguar stylists called the 'jewel look' covering the lenses, along with a chrome ring round the cluster. The bulbous rear bumper had been slightly smoothed out, there was a larger pair of chrome-tipped exhaust pipes, and the low-mounted front fog lamps were now flush-mounted in the moulding, rather than recessed.

Inside the cabin, also shared with all other XK8s, was what was called the ARTS (adaptive restraint technology system), which used ultrasonic detectors (one in each A or B pillar, and one in the roof-positioned centre console) to work out the position of the front passengers within the cabin, all in aid of providing optimum air bag and seat position actuation in case of an accident. A passenger sitting too close to the facia would find that the air bag would not be actuated (no space for it to do a good job), and if the passenger seat was not occupied it would not be activated either.

All such factors, Jaguar claimed, were fed through the ARTS central processor every ten milliseconds, to determine whether two air bags or one would be deployed partially or fully, depending on the severity of the accident. To add to the security package, front seats had been redesigned to have more support, had side airbags fitted as standard, and the side impact bars in the doors were also stronger than before.

To petrol heads (and there were thousands still looking forward to buying the latest sporty Jaguar) this all sounded very boring – but where specified, none of the other SVO features had been degraded in any detail. 20in alloy wheels, fat tyres (285/30 section at the rear), huge Brembo brakes, cross-drilled disc rotors, firmed up springs and dampers and stiffer anti-roll bars were all still there. At £66,005 for a fully SVO-equipped XKR

Coupé, this was an expensive but beguiling combination.

Into the New Century

Jaguar, however, never lost sight of the way that its market place was changing. In the bad old days, when the company had to rely on its own rather meagre financial resources, there were periods when the dear old XJS had had to be allowed to drift along without improvements, and (in particular in North America) this meant that the company's otherwise faithful clientèle sometimes became bored with the product.

But that was then, and this was…more demanding. One of the XK8's most important head-to-head rivals had always been the Mercedes-Benz SL range (think of sunshine, a rich clientèle, and Rodeo Drive in Los Angeles), and Jaguar knew that it always had to keep up.

For years Browns Lane seemed to manage this with aplomb, but in mid-2001 the arrival of a completely new generation SL changed everything. Behind the three-pointed star there was now a range of 5-litre V8 and 5.4-litre V12 engines, covering 306bhp to 476bhp. Prices were admittedly high, but so were performance and build standards. So what could Jaguar do next?

6 XK180 and F-Type – Even Sportier Concepts

Working in the design studios of a company such as Jaguar must be the most exciting, and at the same time the most frustrating, of activities. Many projects may be discussed and several mock-up cars or even prototypes may be built, but very few ever get into series production. Two famous one-offs that were inspired by the XK8 – one being the XK180, the other the F-Type – are typical of this process.

As I have already made clear, once Ford brought Jaguar back from the brink of financial meltdown in the early 1990s, it then started rebuilding the range for the years to come.

Without Ford's financial support, this could never have been done. As is also clear, the priority of rejuvenating the range of saloons took precedence over work on sports cars, and this also explains why there was so much hardware and heritage from the XJS hidden away under the skin of the XK8. By the late 1990s, though, there was time to breathe, time to look over the design parapet – and time to show the world what Jaguar's designers could actually do.

After Ford had ensured Jaguar's survival and then underpinned its future, it decided to enlarge its specialist team at Browns Lane: thus

The XK180 Concept Roadster, much smaller and lighter than the XK8 from which it was derived, was wickedly attractive.

If only Jaguar had had the money, the courage of its convictions, and full backing from Ford at the time, the 'F-Type' would certainly have gone on sale, and become a success.

evolved the Special Vehicle Operations department, from the operation latterly responsible for assembling the ageing Daimler Limousine, and which would now be charged with what

On the XK180, twin humps behind the passenger seats were an interesting styling point, which might have been modified if Jaguar designers had taken the project further.

might be called 'thinking outside the box'. When offered a challenge and a certain amount of resources, Jaguar's SVO team would have to produce exciting one-offs, or design themes, and it was an operation that any number of staff fought to join.

The XK180

In the meantime, the atmosphere in the Jaguar design studios at Whitley was busy at this time. Work on the revised XJ saloons was virtually complete, the XK8 was well established in production at Browns Lane, and the shaping of the still secret S-Type – to be manufactured at a new facility at Castle Bromwich – was nearly finalized. The XKR was also ready to meet its customers, and now there was time – just a bit of time – to play around with concepts. And so in 1998, the XK180 project sports car was born.

After the usual rush to complete a one-off prototype, the new car, painted in a compelling ice blue shade, was displayed at the Paris Motor Show in October 1998; quite naturally it caused a sensation. However, although it all looked eminently practical, and was a real car as opposed to a wood and plaster mock-up, Jaguar apparently had no plans to put it on sale.

The story, or really the influence behind this car, dates back to the 1950s, when Jaguar's sensational D-Type was at the height of its fame. Here was a sleek, glamorous and effective two-seater, which took the existing Jaguar two-seater sports car image to great heights – and it was this sort of shock result that Jaguar thought they could whimsically replicate forty years on.

Although much of the engineering evolution, and the technical and design themes that went into the new project, was predictable, the choice of a model title was quite inspired. XK180 not only linked the new car with the still new XK8 road car title, but it harked back, proudly, to the XK sports cars that had quite transformed Jaguar's image in the 1940s and 1950s. It was no coincidence that the XK180 was revealed as a one-off 'show car' almost exactly fifty years after the very first XK120 had made its bow.

Like all such projects, the XK180 was born in a 'Why don't we…?' discussion, and was always meant to be an awareness-raiser, rather than the first genuine prototype of a forth-coming car. In the beginning – late in 1997 – Gary Albrighton (principal engineer in SVO) got together with Colin Cook and Howard Davies (of the public affairs and marketing departments) to see how an 'XK120 anniversary' car could be built up.

At first it was intended that this car should concentrate its novelties on its looks, rather than on new engineering, that it should some-how hark back to the D-Type too, and that it should always be based on the platform and mechanical engineering of the still secret XKR model. In the beginning, the team was hoping to get away with making modifications to an existing XK8 convertible, which might have been given a lowered windscreen and perhaps even a tail fin! Such a car might have looked awkward, but once senior designer Keith Helfet got involved and cast his experienced eye over the proposals, this all changed. Almost overnight, it seemed, the 'Why don't we…?' idea turned into a much more serious project car design study, and what we now know as the XK180 was born.

By almost any standards, here was a car that came together at breakneck speed – especially from a company not exactly overstaffed with engineers and designers, and especially as the first (and only) prototype of the V12, mid-engined, four-wheel-drive XJ220 supercar was also taking shape, a shape in which Helfet had already been intimately involved. Jaguar later confirmed that it took only forty-two weeks to turn the first discussions into a real car, forty-two hectic weeks in which the basic mechanical layout of the machine was agreed, in which Keith Helfet and his colleagues produced a stunning two-seater style, in which a 'mule' (an XK8 Convertible) was chopped about to turn the running gear into a facsimile of what would eventually appear, and in which the first car was completed.

With the approval of his design boss, Geoff Lawson, Helfet concentrated on getting the shape right before the engineering could be finalized. Almost immediately it became clear that a style that paid homage to the D-Type would not work, for this fantastic old car had had longer front and rear overhangs, neither of which would sit comfortably on the basis of the rather stubbier XK8 platform. In the end, the team elected to base the car more closely on the existing lines of the XK8, but to achieve them around a two-seater roadster theme, where the wheelbase of the XK8 platform had been reduced by 5in (128mm) – to be precise, from 8ft 5.9in (2,588mm) to 8ft 0.85in (2,460mm): this meant that it would be the shortest-ever iteration of this platform – which still, I remind you, had links to the original pressings to be found under the XJ6 of 1968.

Helfet and his compact team then produced sketch after sketch, before homing in on the shape that startled the world of motoring in Paris. Similar in some of its themes, but different in detail to the XK8 (and, of course, meant to be crafted with light alloy skin panels rather than steel), the XK180 was a much shorter car, a two-seater pure and simple, with no pretensions to being a load-carrying 'family' sports car.

Confirming the truism that: 'The impossible we do at once, but miracles take a little time', it is worth noting the time scale surrounding the naissance of the XK180. Once the initial concept had been agreed in November 1997 and design/styling had begun, it was the shaping of this sensational two-seater, and the crafting of the first car, that took up much time. What we enthusiasts still call 'styling' (these days more properly known as 'design') occupied most of the winter months of 1997/1998, with a definitive full-size clay model taking shape at Loades Design, a sister company of Abbey Panels. Every Jaguar enthusiast will recognize the name of Abbey Panels, for this company had always produced body panels and structures for the C-Type and D-Type racing sports cars, and for the one-off mid-engined XJ13, and was currently heavily involved in the secret XJ220 project.

Approval of the shape of the finalized clay model came in April 1998, and body-shell fabrication began almost at once: it was ready for paint and furnishing by mid-June. Keith Helfet chose a metallic blue paint job, which some say harked back to the colour used on Ecurie Ecosse D-Types in the 1950s, but with modern traces of green and gold! Interior design occupied June, July and August, the car was finally made ready for photography in mid-September 1998, and it was finally launched at the end of that month.

An enormous amount of effort went into the styling of the new car. Shorter, slightly wider, and altogether stubbier than the XK8/XKR, the new car was as compact a 450bhp two-seater as Jaguar's designers could make it, for both front and rear shapes were sinuously attenuated. Without any extraneous mouldings, and with overhangs almost 4in (100mm) shorter than on standard cars, the XK180 ended up no less than 12.8in/325mm shorter than the standard road cars.

As it would be next to impossible to describe the exterior shape without much waving of hands and gestures, this is where illustrations are all important. Although the nose looked somewhat like the XK8/XKR, there were simpler oval headlamp covers instead of the

Quite a number of detail features on the XK180 show cars were derived from the XKR, such as the louvres in the bonnet, the front spoiler and the mesh grille.

Like the F-Type that was to follow, the XK180 had a very simple instrument panel display, though every possible control and gauge was present. Note the very special seats, the aluminium foot rest ahead of the passenger, and the traditional J-gate arrangement of automatic transmission selector controls on the transmission tunnel.

Compare and contrast this view of the XK180 project car with the F-Type that would follow less than two years afterwards. The two cars were similar in so many ways.

rather complex contours of the road car, the windscreen and the windows in the doors were lower and frameless, there were twin humps behind the two seats, and at the extreme tail there was a transverse spoiler rather similar to that seen on the XJ220 supercar.

Amazingly, although there were absolutely no shared panels, or even shared profiles, between the two types, the XK180 reminded everyone instantly of the XK8/XKR from which it was derived. It would only be when the two cars were posed side by side that the complete difference became apparent.

Inside the cockpit, of course, the treatment was unique, with a blend of tooled aluminium, leather trim facings and specially trimmed Recaro racing-type seats, with full racing safety-belt harnesses to match. To prove that this car was all about making an impression, rather than preparing the way for a production car, on this project car Jaguar had made no attempt to provide wind-down windows, air conditioning, a sound system, windscreen wipers, air bags, or a fold-away soft top! The car revealed for the Paris show was a right-hand-drive machine; a second car (or was it the same project car, completely reworked?) was in left-hand drive, and first seen at the Detroit Motor Show in January 1999.

In some ways, mechanical design had been a simpler process. Once the decision had been taken to shorten the XK8 platform, but to retain the same basic running gear, the details rapidly fell into place. The engine itself was a more powerful derivative of the supercharged XKR8 power unit, the wheels were sexy 20in alloys (those of the XKR were 18in types) with even wider rims, and the brakes were enlarged to look after the increased performance. The Mercedes-Benz-supplied five-speed automatic gearbox was retained.

It was the detail behind all these basics that made so much difference. The engine could only have been boosted from 376bhp (XKR) to 450bhp by forcing more air-fuel mixture through the 4-litre unit, and this had been done by increasing the rotating speed of the Eaton supercharger, at the same time making the air/air intercooler much larger: the surface area was enhanced by a massive 81 per cent, which was difficult to accommodate under the sleek skin. There was also different inlet and exhaust manifolding, a new larger bore exhaust system, and no exhaust catalysts to impede the passage of exhaust gases. (Since Jaguar had no intention of putting this particular car on sale, there was no need for it to meet the latest, very stringent, exhaust emissions regulations. A production version, of course, would have had to have catalysts included, and that power rating would have been reduced accordingly.)

Brought into the project at an early stage, Mercedes-Benz had to take a deep breath before refining their five-speed automatic transmission to deal with the enhanced power output – but as the same transmission was already having to cope with the 394bhp/6-litre V12 power of the 600SL production sports car (and that company's tuning experts, AMG, could produce even more power than this), they soon found ways of making it reliable. Once again, since this particular transmission did not have to go into series production, a few corners could be taken, and some special components were also used.

Not only was a modified version of Jaguar's now traditional 'J-gate' transmission ratio-change lever retained on the tunnel, but in this case that lever was linked to the 'manual', or sequential change facility, by way of twin buttons on spokes of the steering wheel.

To match all this power and these intermediate ratios to the potential performance of the car, the final drive ratio was raised to 2.88:1 (from 3.06:1 on the XKR). Although the top speed of this amazing machine was apparently never established, it was thought that it might have been 180mph (290km/h),

which is one way of explaining the new car's title, and Jaguar was also insistent that it could sprint from rest to 100mph (160km/h) in no more than 10sec.

Except that the propeller shaft had to be shortened to match up to the 5in (13cm) shortening of the platform, the rest of the chassis differed from the XKR in detail, rather than in any of its basics. After much testing on a 'mule' (described below), the suspension and damping rates were modified, the dampers being adjustable gas-filled Bilsteins from Germany (this company being renowned for its rally-car damping systems) and fitted with height-adjustment collars.

Except for local upgrades, front and rear suspension geometry and componentry were standard XKR; front and rear anti-roll bars were both stiffened up, and vast race-/rally-developed Brembo brakes, with four-pot aluminium callipers at front and rear, were fitted inside the larger, 20in diameter alloy wheels. Higher-geared steering was proposed, but had not yet been fitted when the car was first shown in public.

All this was tested in an old XK8/XKR 'mule', while the styling of the new project was being finalized – and it was that particular car that caused confusion when the project went public. At once more practical, but significantly more utilitarian than the XK180 itself, this was the first running 'look-see' for the project car, being based on a hastily chopped, re-welded and reassembled XK8 convertible, which retained the existing front end and back end style, though the platform was 5in shorter, the fillet having been taken out behind the doors, and at the same time the rear 'plus two' seats were removed.

To help stiffen up the structure (and to make very high-speed motoring feel that bit more secure for the test team) a solid roll cage was welded into place, there being no attempt to keep the soft top on this car. Almost everything that would appear on the show cars was first tried out on this machine: it was noticeable that this was the first of these machines

---

Jaguar XK180 Project Car

Specification as for XK8 of the period, except for:		4th	1.00
		3rd	1.41
Layout	Unit construction body/chassis structure, with steel underpan/platform and aluminium skin panels, two-seater, only built as a show car	2nd	2.19
		1st	3.59:1
		Reverse	3.15:1
		Final drive ratio	2.88:1

Suspension and steering

Engine	
Compression ratio	9.0:1
Fuel supply	Nippondenso fuel injection/engine management system, with Eaton supercharger, maximum boost 0.8 bar
Max. power	450bhp (DIN)
Max. torque	445lb.ft

Tyres	(F) 255/35ZR-20in, (R) 285/30ZR-20in., radial ply
Wheels	Cast aluminium disc, bolt-on
Rim width	(F) 9in, (R) 10in

Brakes

Transmission	Automatic transmission (Mercedes-Benz type) standard. Ratio selection by tunnel-mounted 'J-gate', or by twin buttons mounted on the steering-wheel spokes
Type	Disc brakes at front and rear, with vacuum servo assistance and anti-lock
Size	14in/355mm diameter front, 12.4in/315mm diameter rear

Dimensions (in/mm)

Internal Ratios	
Top/5th	0.83
Wheelbase	96.85/2,460
Overall length	182.5in/4,635mm
Overall width	79.3in/2,015mm (no mirrors)
Overall height	50.6in/1,285mm
Unladen weight	3,438lb/1,560kg

---

that would use a front-end nose spoiler to help cut down on front-end lift at speeds of 150mph (240km/h) and more: the stylists did not like the look of this, but agreed that it was better to have a supercar that stayed on the ground, than one that tended to take off. Later, a more deeply moulded front spoiler was added to the XK180 itself, along with a different transverse rear spoiler and a full length undertray.

Then it all went quiet. As far as I can see, neither car was ever seriously tested by anyone in the media, performance figures were neither taken nor published, and although the cars were much demonstrated in 1999, little further development appears to have been done and

they eventually went back into store. Even so, apart from the immeasurable publicity gained by their launch and display, much of the technical knowledge gained in modifying the XK8 chassis and running gear to XK180 specifications could be turned to the long-term improvement of the XK8 itself.

F-Type

Soon after the XK180 appeared, flared into prominence and was then committed to retirement, an even more exciting XK8 derivative, the F-Type, was developed. At this stage, though, I must immediately point out that the 'F-Type', as seen by the public, shared no

The launch of the F-Type in 2000 caused a sensation, all the pundits loved it, and it would surely have been a success if put on sale.

Not a line, curve or detail out of place — the short-wheelbase F-Type as shown off in 2000.

mechanical components with the XK180, though the styling of the two cars was clearly related. Accordingly, the F-Type is only of marginal interest to the XK8 story.

At the time, every Jaguar enthusiast was convinced that a production car would evolve from the show car, Jaguar's publicity machine was happy to support them in this assumption, and work indeed forged ahead – until Ford suddenly cancelled the project, citing a financial squeeze and a shortage of resources. At the time, cancellation looked like an act of folly – and even today many observers wonder if Jaguar took leave of their senses, lost their collective nerve, or simply did not understand what their market was really crying out for, particularly in the USA. Whatever the case, the fact is that the new F-Type was developed, launched, analysed – and abruptly cancelled. It was a classic case of 'What if…?'

First thoughts on an 'F-Type' came early in 1999 (not long after the XK180 project cars took to the road, in fact). Public reaction to the XK180, though encouraging, had always shown an undercurrent that harked back to the

Although there was a strong family resemblance to the XKR production car, and to the XK180 it succeeded, the detail shaping of the F-Type concept was unique.

If the F-Type concept had gone forwards to become a production two-seater, changes would almost certainly have been made to the rear style and to the cockpit surround.

The F-Type concept's facia/instrument/control layout was stark and purposeful. It would almost certainly have been 'softened up' when a production version was made.

The XK180 might only have been a concept car, but it handled like a Jaguar thoroughbred.

Was Jaguar wise to restrict the XK180 theme to a single concept car? Decide for yourselves.

Maybe heavier and bulkier than the E-Type had been in the 1960s, the F-Type would certainly have been a worthy successor to that iconic Jaguar sports car.

legendary E-Type of 1961–1975, and there seemed to be a groundswell opinion that future Jaguar sports cars should at once be smaller, lighter and (if possible) cheaper than before.

As noted, the F-Type project car (an unfinished styling mock-up) made its bow at the Detroit Motor Show in January 2000, where it was advertised as having a V6 engine (as was to be used in the X-Type saloon), all independent suspension, and a six-speed sequential-change manual transmission. None of these features was ever shown to the public (it seems that the car shown was never completed), and the car then disappeared back into Jaguar's design/development HQ for further work to take place.

Final F-Type Upheaval

Suddenly, in August 2001, a controlled leak in *Autocar* magazine told an astonished world that the original F-Type layout had been ditched in favour of a new transverse-engined rear/mid-engined layout instead! The reader can imagine, I am sure, the technical, functional and financial upheaval that this had caused at Whitley, for it meant that all the work so far done on XK8-inspired F-Types was to be wasted.

The new-type F-Type – we might call it the F-Type Mk 2 – was given the Jaguar project code of X600, and at that time the launch was forecast for 2005. Much of the project work had already been done, it seems, and much had been learned from mid-engined prototypes built up by Aston. A much smaller car than the original F-Type, it was also to be significantly lighter and powered by V6 engines as already in use in the X-Type and S-Type saloons.

Jaguar, of course, tried to shrug off this leak as speculation (although the information had come from within the concern), but behind the scenes the truth seems to be that work on the original front-engine X-Type 'Mark 1' project had already been wound down; it is at this point, therefore, that our interest in an F-Type should end.

Within a year, in any case, the usual Ford/Jaguar financial constraints (which seemed to be endemic throughout the decade) hit hard at this car, which was itself cancelled, and has never been seen since.

7   4.2 Litres – More Performance, Same Style, Final Maturity

Perhaps Jaguar would never admit it, neither now nor in the past, but work on the XK180 and F-Type concept cars had taken up a great deal of their time at Whitley. Company insiders, and company rivals alike, both agree that Jaguar was trying to achieve so much at this time that certain urgently needed programmes had to wait, and maybe even see their programme schedules slip.

Following the successful build-up of both sales and reputation of XK8 derivatives such as the XKR, the Silverstone and the SVO derivatives, Jaguar's management wanted to take a good long look at the entire range of sporty cars, and to produce a revised line-up. This would not merely be a facelift, but a thorough and thoughtful mid-life update. It was something that any professional car-maker undertook – all the dealers expected it, all the rivals expected it, and everyone understood that it meant that work on a major replacement model was already being considered.

If more resources had been available – not only financial, but a bigger pool of experienced engineers – and if other new Jaguar models had not needed to be launched in the

Even when surrounded by piping and ducts, the supercharged AJ-V8 (this is, in fact, a 4.2-litre version, as fitted to the S-Type of the early 2000s) was a very neat and purposeful-looking piece of engineering.

High-speed, top down, and fine weather on the West Coast of the USA – what could be more enjoyable?

A 2003 XKR shows the very delicate retouching made in 2002 when the 4.2-litre engine appeared, and when even larger road wheels were fitted.

Well over 400bhp was available from the XKR engine, in supercharged form, when enlarged to 4.2-litres in 2002.

same period, then a revised XK8 might have appeared as early as 2000 – but as it was, there would be no sign of any such cars until the summer of 2002.

Starting with the appearance of the XK, this simple chart of Jaguar new-product action shows why:

March 1998	Launch of XKR, complete with supercharged engine
October 1998	Preview of new S-Type saloons, NEC Motor Show
October 1998	Launch of XK180 two-seater concept car
Spring 1999	S-Type went into production at Castle Bromwich
January 2000	Launch of F-Type two-seater

When the package of improvements including the 4.2-litre engine were unveiled, Jaguar posed the three cars that would all benefit from the upgrade: the XKR (right), the S-Type and the XJ saloon.

February 2001   Launch of new four-wheel-drive X-Type saloon range, at Halewood (Merseyside), the ex-Ford Escort production plant

March 2002   Launch of much-revised S-Type saloons, the first Jaguars to use the revised 4.2-litre V8 engine

This, I think, demonstrates why there was only so much that Jaguar's engineers, planners and production staff could do. The design, engineering and styling centre at Whitley was at full stretch throughout this time, so it was no wonder that work on changes and improvements to the relatively slow-selling XK8/XKR models would have to wait their turn. The XK8 was, maybe, a high-profile model in the range, and

the XKR was the fastest – but the accountants, as ever, had a bottom line to consider.

Although the much hoped-for improvements to XK8/XKR finally came in the spring of 2002 – soon after the S-Type received its own mid-term facelift, in fact – by that time Jaguar watchers had already worked out what *might* be going to happen. Looking back at that chart, there's little doubt that the arrival of an improved S-Type saloon, complete with a 4.2-litre engine and a six-speed automatic transmission, was most significant.

More Torque, More Capacity, More Ratios

With the XK8 and XKR selling well, and still looking as good as ever, no attempt had been made to do any restyling work to the cars. Although a true XK8 fanatic could look

By 2002 the Jaguar range comprised four basically different models: left to right the X-Type, the XJ saloons, the XK8 and the S-Type. The XK8, of course, was built on its own unique platform.

Jaguar XK8 (from 2002)

Layout	Unit-construction steel body/chassis structure. 2+2-seater, front engine/rear drive, sold as two-door closed coupé or cabriolet	1st	4.17:1
		Reverse	3.40:1
		Final drive ratio	3.31:1

Engine

Type	Jaguar AJ-V8
Block material	Cast aluminium
Head material	Cast aluminium
Cylinders	8 in 90-degree V
Cooling	Water
Bore and stroke	86 × 90.3mm
Capacity	4196cc
Main bearings	5
Valves	4 per cylinder, operated by twin-overhead camshafts per cylinder heads, with hydraulic phasing of cam timing, and inverted bucket-type tappets
Compression ratio	11.0:1
Fuel supply	Nippondenso fuel injection/engine management system
Max. power	300bhp (DIN) @ 6,000rpm
Max. torque	303lb.ft @ 4,100rpm

Transmission

	Manual gearbox not available. Automatic transmission (ZF type – 6HP26) standard

Internal Ratios

Top/6th	0.69
5th	0.87
4th	1.14
3rd	1.32
2nd	2.34

Suspension and steering

Front	Independent, coil springs, wishbones, anti-roll bar, telescopic dampers
Rear	Independent, double coil springs, fixed-length drive shafts, lower wishbones, radius arms, twin telescopic dampers
Steering	Rack-and-pinion, power-assisted, 2.8 turns lock-to-lock
Tyres	245/50ZR-17in, radial ply
Wheels	Cast aluminium disc, bolt-on
Rim width	8in

Brakes

Type	Disc brakes at front and rear, with vacuum servo assistance and anti-lock
Size	12.8in/325mm diameter front, 12in/305mm diameter rear

Dimensions (in/mm)

Track	Front 59.2/1,504
	Rear 59.0/1,498
Wheelbase	101.9/2,588
Overall length	187.4/4,760
Overall width (incl mirrors)	79.3/2,015
Overall height	Coupé 51.0/1,296
	Cabriolet 51.4/1,306
Unladen weight	Coupé 3,715lb/1,685kg
	Cabriolet 3,914lb/1,775kg

---

carefully round and pick out a few minor changes, for 2003 the basic style, and package, was just the same as it had been when launched in 1996. Sheet-metal changes, though perhaps desirable in some aspects of the cars, would have been costly to carry out, and there would also have been delays while those changes were made to the body plant at Castle Bromwich.

Incidentally, and if only we had known it, work on a replacement model for the XK8/XKR was already under way. This, of course, was firmly under wraps – and, by the way, the fact that the next-generation car would look so very much like the existing model was a real credit to it. However, we now know that the new car was to be built in an

This ghosted detail shows how the XJ-V8 engine featured two separate driving chains for the overhead camshafts – one for each cylinder bank – and the 4-valves-per-cylinder layout is also clear.

BELOW: This schematic drawing is an even more detailed version of that shown to the left.

Four different Jaguar models in 2002, with the revised XK8 Convertible alongside the X-Type saloon, both of them behind the XJ8 (bottom left) and S-Type (marginally in the lead) in this staged shot.

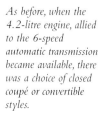

As before, when the 4.2-litre engine, allied to the 6-speed automatic transmission became available, there was a choice of closed coupé or convertible styles.

One thing at once. For 2003, Jaguar introduced the latest 4.2-litre engine and the 6-speed automatic transmission into the XK8 pedigree, but made no important style changes to what had become a classic style.

These high-tech Brembo brakes were standard fittings to the 2003 XKR specification.

Pierced aluminium pedal pads were a feature of the optional 'Aluminium pack' on 2003-model specifications.

Had you forgotten what type of Jaguar you were driving? The XKR had an 'R' type gear change lever knob to remind you.

How many people actually stopped to read the front badge on the 2003 XKR? If they did, the word 'Supercharged' should have reminded them of the 4.2-litre car's awesome potential.

Like all such modern engines, and cars, in 4.2-litre form, the AJ-V8 engine of the latest XK8 was well hidden from inspection by this plastic cover over the inlet manifolds. This was the normally aspirated version.

entirely different way – much bonding and riveting instead of welding, the use of aluminium instead of pressed steel – in other words, there would be virtually no carry over from the past.

And so it was that the latest version of this sleek and handsome model was previewed in March 2002, and went on sale in the summer of 2002. As far as technical information was concerned, Jaguar first of all gave details of the latest car itself, then of the substantial changes made to the engine, the transmission and the rest of the running gear.

Engine Changes

Although the V8 engine was still only six years old, in production terms, constant pressure from rivals, from the Jaguar dealerships and from the clientèle, meant that substantial changes were brought forwards, not only for the XK8/XKR, but for the S-Type, the XJ8 and for upmarket four-wheel-drive models that Land Rover was also developing.

Central to the update was the introduction of a new 4.2-litre version of the existing AJ-V8 engine. As far as the XK8 was concerned, this was a real novelty, though the motoring world had already seen it in the revised S-Type saloon, which had been launched earlier in the year. Ford also planned that the same much-revised V8 would also find a home in future Range Rover models and in the next-generation Jaguar XJ saloons, which were all under development. (Incidentally, I am personally convinced that the choice of 4.2 litres – as opposed to, say, 4.3 litres – was at least partly influenced by the fact that one of Jaguar's classic, though by then outdated, versions of the XK 6-cylinder engine had also been a 4.2-litre!)

All this, I now know, had been preplanned when the engine was at the testing stage in the early 1990s because, as Trevor Crisp later confirmed, there was always the thought that the family might have to be stretched a little to allow the engineers to meet the ever-tightening exhaust emission legislation that continued to flood out of North America, Europe and Japan. This meant that, although the engine itself had been enlarged, from 3996cc to 4196cc, this had been done merely by lengthening the cylinder stroke a little – from 86mm to 90.3mm. Naturally this meant that a new crankshaft was required, but there had been no need to make any changes to the cast cylinder block, or to the existing twin-overhead-camshaft cylinder heads. Jaguar enthusiasts will want to know that, within the company, the latest engine was now known as the AJ34.

All the basic details of the original types – the same constructional, machining and assembly details – were as before, and at this stage it is worth noting that the design had originally been laid out so that V8s of different capacities could eventually be manufactured. Although such units were never to be used in any type of XK8, not even those built for special markets with special taxation regimes, the V8 would also be built in sizes of 3253cc and 3555cc (in each case by the use of special short-stroke crankshafts) – and from late 2004 the first of the Range Rover Sport 4×4s was available with a 'big bore' derivative of the same engine, making a 4394cc capacity. This family's life can be found in the panel on page 65.

Compared with the original 4-litre type, all the advanced features were still there, including the variable inlet camshaft timing, whose actuator was sensed by hydraulic actuators, and an engine control module containing electronic maps of engine speeds and loads; if necessary it could adjust the timing of the camshafts, from maximum advance to maximum retard, in less than 0.7sec.

Among the mass of new detail added to the engine at this juncture were new multi-hole fuel injectors (the better to refine the spray pattern inside the combustion chambers), and an electronic management system that controlled all primary functions including fuel delivery, ignition timing, throttle control, variable cam phasing, exhaust gas recirculation, fuel purging, knock control and actuation of the engine cooling fans. All this, and the 'drive by wire' connection between the throttle pedal and the engine throttles themselves, made this an ultra-sophisticated power unit.

One further change was that on the XKR a further evolution of the Eaton supercharger was standardized, this now having helically profiled rotor gears (this helped reduce noise levels) and coated rotors. At the same time, the drive, via a belt from the front of the crankshaft, was re-geared: this meant that it was rotating 5 per cent faster than before, which helped to boost the peak horsepower.

When completing all the detail work on the V8 engine, including making it larger and ensuring that it could also be modified for use in the Range Rover 4×4s, Jaguar had not merely been looking for a lot more peak power. On the other hand, more torque at all points and – equally important – more refinement allied to reduced exhaust emissions were thought to be vital. As fitted to the XK8/XKR models, this, therefore, is how the original 4-litre engines compared with the latest 4.2-litre types:

Size (and year introduced)	Peak power bhp @ rpm	Peak torque lb.ft @ rpm
3996cc (1996 – XK8)	290 @ 6,100	290 @ 4,250
3996cc (1998 – XKR)	376 @ 6,150	387 @ 3,600
4196cc (2002 – XK8)	300 @ 6,000	303 @ 4,100
4196cc (2002 – XKR)	400 @ 6,100	408 @ 3,500

The most significant advance was that, on the XKR, peak power had been increased by 8 per cent, while peak torque was up by 5.4 per cent without increasing the revs at which this was developed.

Compared with the original supercharged engine fitted to the XKR of 1998–2002, the installation of the Eaton-supercharged 4.2-litre unit of 2002/2003 was virtually identical.

Jaguar XKR (from September 2002)

Specification as for the 4.2-litre XK8 of September 2002 onwards, except for:

Engine

Bore and stroke	86 × 90.3mm
Capacity	4196cc
Compression ratio	9.1:1
Fuel supply	Nippondenso fuel injection/ engine management system, with Eaton-type supercharger boosting to 0.8bar
Max. power	400bhp (DIN) @ 6,100rpm
Max. torque	408lb.ft @ 3,500rpm

Suspension and steering

Tyres	(F) 245/45ZR-18in, (R) 255/45ZR-18in, radial ply
Wheels	Cast aluminium disc, bolt-on
Rim width	(F) 8in, (R) 9in

Brakes

Size	14in/355mm diameter front, 12.6in/320mm diameter rear

Dimensions

Unladen weight	Coupé 3,826lb/1,735kg Cabriolet 4,002lb/1,815kg

One had to look hard at the 2004 XK8, as launched in May 2004, to see the visual changes that had been made. At the front of the car, on the XK8, there was a larger front bumper moulding. The over-riders were retained, but not, of course, on the XKR.

From May 2004 the XKR looked even more butch than before. Not only did it have the bulkier front bumper that it shared with the XK8, but from the front it was also possible to see the new mesh front grille, a deep sculpted front spoiler and the more prominent side skirts.

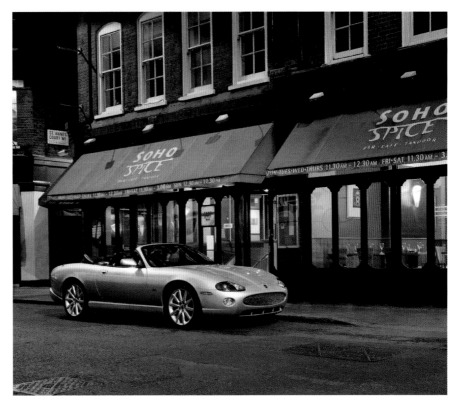

What really irritated Jaguar's rivals was that a sporting car like the XK8 could look like a million-dollar machine, but still sell at such a reasonable price. In May 2004, in the UK, the XK8 Convertible sold for just £56,720.

When the 2004 XKR was in motion, it certainly looked even more purposeful, not to say menacing, than before. There was still plenty of ground clearance under the new front spoiler, and all those air intakes were certainly needed to keep the 395bhp supercharged engine well cooled.

The brave driver has got this 2004 model XKR, complete with 20in wheels and tyres, well sideways on a treacherous surface. There isn't anything superfluous in the XKR of this vintage.

The 2004 XKR featured a bigger and more brawny rear bumper moulding (all the better to hide the new tail pipes), and those vast Pirelli P-Zero 285/30ZR20 tyres (on 9in wide front rims, and 10in wide rear rims) were a very desirable option.

139

Six Forward Speeds

It was in the automatic transmission for the rejuvenated XK8 that ZF had really excelled themselves. Knowing that their principal client (BMW) wanted to go to a six-speed automatic, and suspecting that Mercedes-Benz would soon be producing their own-brand six-speeder, ZF buckled down and developed a six-speed derivative of the original five-speeder, which had been brand new when first seen in 1996. Not only that, but ZF's new six-speeder would be strong enough to deal with the XKR's torque delivery too, so Jaguar would no longer have to be a customer of Mercedes-Benz, who were still rivals.

This new transmission was quite phenomenally smooth and cultured in everything it did (the author has used an unrelated type of German car with the same six-speeder fitted, and can vouch for it), and made it even less likely that there would be any complaints from Jaguar die-hards who might otherwise want what American buyers called a 'stick shift'.

Not that this was merely the old five-speeder (whose fourth gear had been 'direct drive') with an 'overdrive' six-speeder grafted into the tail. ZF, thorough as ever, had started from the beginning again, for this was now an all-indirect installation. Here is a comparison of internal ratios:

ZF five-speed: 0.8, 1.00, 1.51, 2.20, 3.57, reverse 4.1:1. Final drive ratio 3.06:1
ZF six-speed: 0.69/0.87, 1.14, 1.32, 2.32, 4.17, reverse 3.4:1. Final drive ratio 3.31:1

This, incidentally, meant that in top/sixth ratio, the overall gearing was 40mph (64km/h)/1,000rpm, compared with a rather more frantic 32mph (51km/h)/1,000rpm with the old five-speed transmission.

Of this new gearbox, as installed in a companion Jaguar, one respected motoring writer commented:

> The real revelation is just how well the new 4.2-litre V8 works with that ZF six-speed automatic gearbox. With a little more engine displacement than the old 4.0-litre, and a longer stroke, the idea was to improve the V8's power and response right through the rev range, particularly at the lower end. When you combine that with a gearbox with sensible ratios – and lots of them – which kicks down exactly when you need it to, the resulting performance is hugely impressive.
>
> The result is wonderfully smooth, with changes that slur luxuriously at about the 6,000rpm mark when you push a bit harder.

Another writer had this to say:

> And that six-speed box complements the engine well. Even when left in Drive, it's as eager to change down on the approach to a bend as it is to maximize the revs (in Sport mode) as you accelerate out of it. While it does, you also appreciate how quick, yet fluid, all the changes are. Few slush-boxes on the market are as enjoyable to use as this.

No wonder Jaguar seemed to be content with the same combination and had therefore installed it in the latest iteration of the XK8.

On the Market

Surprisingly, XK8 sales had been gradually slipping down for some time. This was not a failing of the XK8/XKR itself, but the entire market place seemed to be suffering slightly at this time. A total of 6,127 XK8s and 4,608 XKRs had been produced in 2001 (this was a creditable figure, but still slightly less than any of the previous four years), whereas in 2002, when 4.2-litre types took over for the second half of the year, 4,113 XK8s and 2,748 XKRs were produced.

The downward trend was somewhat worrying, but another one, the emphasis on drop-top sales compared with hard-top coupé sales, was more satisfying. Jaguar had spent an inordinate amount of time making sure that the open cars had stiff shells, and that they would be extremely civilized when used in warm climates, such as most of North America. In the end, as we now know, far more open-top cars were sold than originally forecast – no fewer than 61,058 cars, or 67 per cent of the nine-year total.

With funds as tight as always, Jaguar had not been able to provide the major facelift their designers might have liked. At a casual glance, there was little novelty to be remarked, for there were no sheet-metal changes of any type. Hidden away was a new type of rear-axle differential, and a new electronic stability control which, in certain circumstances, could control unwonted slides by applying individual brakes and cutting the throttle. Emergency brake assist was also new, and the radar-controlled adaptive cruise control now included an audible warning to alert the driver if traffic ahead was already slowing down.

The refinement of this, and the other chassis details, was partly eased by the expertise (for the latest sophisticated Range Rover) that had suddenly become available when Ford bought Land Rover from BMW in 2000.

Detail style and equipment changes included a redesigned Jaguar 'J-gate' automatic transmission selector (six forward speeds instead of five made this desirable), there was new detail around the headlamps and the driving lamps, which were, as ever, retained in the front moulding below those headlamps, and on the 400bhp XKR there was now a new rear badge to mark the upgrade. Add to all this the four new paint colours, and Jaguar could boast – as indeed they did – that there were 900 changes or new parts in the latest range.

And not only that, but there were no price increases, which meant that, as earlier in 2002, the XK8 coupé price was still £48,700, which was still something of a performance bargain, while the most expensive version, the XKR Convertible, cost £63,350. With this car, however, and because of the market sector in which it sat, Jaguar's problem was that the XK8/XKR models were now beginning to look just a little…old.

The latest engine and transmission combination might indeed have made a remarkable

XK8 Production Figures 1996 to 2005					
Calendar year	XK8 Coupé	XK8 Convertible	XKR Coupé	XKR Convertible	Total
1995	8	12	20		
1996	2,925	4,187	7,112		
1997	5,141	9,765	11	12	14,929
1998	3,319	7,662	1,402	838	13,221
1999	1,701	6,196	1,530	1,994	11,421
2000	1,514	5,907	1,778	3,042	12,241
2001	1,723	4,404	1,659	2,949	10,735
2002	1,203	2,910	1,053	1,695	6,861
2003	985	2,280	936	1,455	5,656
2004	627	2,003	708	1,075	4,413
2005	666	1,687	669	985	4,007
Grand Totals	19,812	47,013	9,746	14,045	90,616

According to Jaguar's own records, production of series production (as opposed to 'pilot production') cars got under way in February 1996. The very last XK8/XKR was produced on 27 May 2005.

Sales of XK8s in the USA, 1997 to 2006

If the XK8/XKR series had not sold so well in the USA, it would never have been a viable project. Here are the authentic year-on-year sales figures:

Year	Cars sold (all types)
1997	10,045
1998	8,085
1999	6,976
2000	6,729
2001	5,137
2002	3,935
2003	2,905
2004	2,806
2005	2,282
2006	1,148★
Total	50,048

★(these were left-over stocks, for production had ended in 2005)

---

difference to the way the cars performed, but the style had not changed at all. XK8s built for 2003 and onwards, in other words, still looked just as they had done seven years earlier, and the clientèle had begun to grumble about this. Porsche, for sure, never seemed to change the outline of their 911, but Jaguar did not consider that model as a direct rival – it was their *real* rivals who produced more frequent visual novelties. As one critique made it clear:

> Waftability has always been a Jaguar staple, and this XK is no different. It goes like this: twist the key, slide her into D, and then just tweak your toe for

In the 2000s, the trendies were always going to give Jaguar a hard time because of the styling of the facia/instrument panel. Too old-fashioned for some, too unJaguar-like for others? Make up your own minds. This was the layout of the 2002–03 models, naturally with the J-gate for the six-speed automatic – and, by the way, a speedometer reading up to 180mph (290km/h), which the XKR might have reached if its top speed had not been electronically limited.

Like it or not, the 2004-model XK8/XKR had a well equipped, neatly packaged facia/instrument panel.

Every picture tells a story. In 2004, not only did the XKR get a larger version of the new tail spoiler, but there were four exhaust tailpipes to provide their own distinctive rumbly-rumbly noise. The rear bumper moulding was bigger, too.

The final retouching of what had become a classic design came in March 2005, when what Jaguar called the '4.2S' derivative appeared. Mechanically this car had not changed, but there was a new range of metallic paints – this car being in Satin Silver – and split-rim BBS road wheels.

lashings of supercharger whine and thrust. No gear changes, but no worries either. The ZF slush-matic serves to remind just how exceptional modern auto boxes are, and how much a slick transmission can lift an otherwise ageing pack-age…. The Jaguar now has something of the feel that characterized large Bentleys back in the mid-

1990s: easy to criticize in just about everything it does, bar the exceptional gearbox. It convinces you that obsolete can mean charming, rather than plain old.

This was stirring and, let's be honest, argu-mentative stuff, but Jaguar was happy to grin,

Salt or snow? Not that it seemed to matter to the last of the XK8 range, which was as sure-footed as any two-wheel-drive could possibly be.

Evening light, a hairpin, and a Mediterranean climate – in 2005, even after nine years the XK range was still looking handsome.

be polite, and get on with selling just as many 4.2-litre cars as they could, particularly in the USA where this model was still seen as the most desirable of the current range.

Although we certainly were not sure at the time, once the 4.2-litre/six-speed version of the XK8 and XKR models had been put on sale, most of Jaguar's attention then turned to work on a total replacement of this successful range. This, the car we now know as the new-generation XK (note that the '8' part of the title had been dropped) would finally break cover before the end of 2005.

Even so, Jaguar's sales and marketing departments were not content to let the existing car carry on without any further attention, so several final makeovers were planned. The first of these duly appeared in the spring of 2004, there would be another (the '4.2S' variety) a year later, and true 'special editions' also signalled that a complete replacement was finally due.

Class of 2004

When the 2004 makeover of the XK series finally broke cover in the spring of 2004, Jaguar described it like this:

> The XK's iconic looks have been given a more contemporary feel with the addition of a revised nose and rear section, complemented by new side sills, wheels and trim. The XKR also gets a new mesh grille, supplemented by a lower 'mouth profile' in the front bumper. All Jaguar XK buyers (excluding North America and Japan) will now have the option of increasing the specification of their car by choosing new Premium and Technology packs [though 'Technology' was not to be available in North America and Japan].
>
> These optional packs will greatly increase specification over a standard car, by combining desirable extras such as reverse park control, sports seats, larger wheels and revised interior trim, into an optional package at a significantly reduced price. A new automatic speed limiter is added to the wide range of electronic systems already standard across the XK range to further enhance the driver's ease.

The point was made that the XK8 had already established itself as the best-selling sports car in Jaguar's history, and would carry on. The XJS had outsold the charismatic E-Type, and although well over 100,000 XJSs had been built, it had taken twenty-one years to achieve that figure. As we now know, the XK8/XKR would not outsell the XJS in total, but in terms of cars sold per year, it was certainly the most successful.

Although the basic shape, package and character of these cars was not changed for 2004, the design/styling departments had been able

In 2005, special edition 4.2S XKR models were treated to a sporty set of carbon-fibre veneer coverings for the facia/instrument panel...

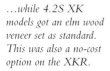

...while 4.2S XK models got an elm wood veneer set as standard. This was also a no-cost option on the XKR.

Who said that 150mph performance could only be provided in a starkly-equipped car, with an impossibly hard ride? The 2004-model XK8 proved otherwise.

to bring forwards a number of visual retouches. First of all there was a new style mesh grille, allied to deeper front and rear 'bumper' mouldings, all adding to more obvious side sills under the doors, which Jaguar claimed improved the aerodynamic performance. For the first time, a transverse rear spoiler was now standardized on the XK8, while that fitted to the XKR was larger than before.

To emphasize the changes, and to remind everyone of the higher performance of the 4.2-litre cars, XK8s were given larger exhaust tail-pipe finishers, while the mighty XKR was given four tail-pipe finishers for the first time. Not only that, but there were three new road wheel styles: Aris (18in), Atlas (19in) and BBS

Sepang (20in). These, incidentally, were added to the existing Gemini (17in), Hydra (18in), BBS Montreal (20in) and Detroit (also 20in) wheel options – consider the stocking problems associated with no fewer than seven wheel types to accommodate! To top all this off, there was now to be a choice of fifteen body colours, eleven of them metallic, which emphasized just how flexible the Jaguar production process had become, along with new interior wood veneers and the option packs already mentioned.

One new electronic feature that seems to have been approved by the 'nanny state' of many territories is that there was now an electronic ASL, or 'automatic speed limiter' device,

Convertible or Coupé – as ever, there was a choice of either with the limited edition/final model of 2005.

For the 'S' final models, the famous XK badge was slightly changed. The XKR retained its 'Supercharged' script, and in addition there was a chequered flag motif.

Fearsomely effective: the combination of cross-drilled ventilated disc rotors and Brembo disc calipers all helped to keep the 400bhp of supercharged XKR performance in check.

which prevented the car from exceeding a pre-selected maximum speed. As an update and an additional feature of cruise control – which was, of course, continued – this driver-set control made it impossible for him to break his own preset limits, until or unless he personally deactivated it or, surprisingly, applied full kick-down via the throttle pedal.

The style changes had emphatically made an important difference, even though there had been no significant sheet-metal changes (which would have cost a small fortune in retooling charges). Front, rear and side bumpers and mouldings had all been modified enough for existing XK8/XKR owners to look, study and nod sagely to themselves. Jaguar, of course, hoped that their reaction would eventually be to visit their dealer to order a new car. The new front-end moulding and more obvious spoiler might have been visually more aggressive and more effective, but it was also demonstrably closer to the ground, as anyone who drove the latest XK too briskly over 'sleeping policemen' in our anti-motorists' towns and cities soon found out.

When it came to 'loading up' the specification through option packs, Jaguar had learned a lot from their masters and from seeing how rivals such as Mercedes-Benz and BMW went about the same business of adding features (and reaping more profits!). The latest XKR was already a well equipped car, of course, but more was included in the Premium pack: the new 19in 'Atlas' style of wheels (and 20in BBS wheels could be optional on this option pack), reverse park radar control, heated front windscreen, Recaro sports seats, cross-drilled brake discs, sports steering wheel, Momo gear-selector knob, a seat-positioning memory pack, aluminium J-gate gear-selector surround, piano black veneer on the facia/instrument board (with burr walnut optional to this pack), and a cup holder.

For the XK customer who wanted to spend time in a comfortable chair in the dealer's showroom before finalizing his order, he could instead choose from individual R-Performance

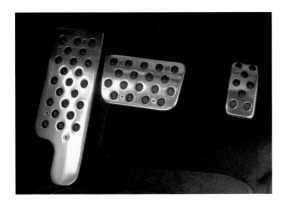

On the S derivatives of 2005, drilled light-alloy pedal pads were a nice touch.

Although some drivers never troubled themselves with the various gearchange options on the XK8 – 'stick it into D' seemed to be a popular option – but as with all XK8s, to achieve the optimum performance, the famous 'J-Gate' layout made it possible to change gear ratios manually.

options, most of which would otherwise be grouped in the Premium pack.

It was interesting to see how time, and the competition, had changed the price levels of these cars, with this simple little chart telling its own story:

Model	British retail price (spring 2004)
Jaguar XK8 Coupé	£49,920
Jaguar XK8 Convertible	£56,720
Jaguar XKR Coupé	£58,120
Jaguar XKR Convertible	£64,920

…while this was the price of rival Mercedes Benz cars:

SL500	£72,160
SL55 AMG	£95,990
SL600	£95,430

By this time the 8-Series BMW had been discontinued, and the Aston Martin DB7 had recently come to the end of a successful run.

All this was enough to keep demand for the XK8 ticking over. A total of 5,656 cars – allowing for holidays and the summer 'shutdown', that equated to about 120 cars every week – had been produced in 2003, and this figure slipped back very slightly to 4,413 cars (ninety-two every week) in 2004. The market place, it seemed, realized that the XK8, now approaching its tenth birthday, would no longer change, except in detail.

Final Fling

Suddenly, in January 2005, all but the most naive of sports car enthusiasts realized that the end was in sight for the XK8, as Jaguar announced the advanced lightweight coupé (ALC) concept car, which looked amazingly like a comprehensive redesign of the old car. It was, in fact, much more than this, for it had an all-aluminium body shell, styling changes in all areas, and was significantly lighter and more modern in its detail than the existing XK8.

The ALC was, in fact, nothing more or less than a coat-trailing exercise for the forthcoming XK, which would make its official debut much later in the year, and which took over from the XK8/XKR range. To show how much change was made, I have provided a final, short chapter (following this one) showing just how much Jaguar had learned from a decade of XK8 manufacture.

In the meantime, and to keep the pot boiling, as it were, two more innovations were planned for the final months of the existing car's career. In Europe, and announced at the Geneva Motor Show in March, the final 'special edition' of the XK8/XKR became the 4.2S type, while in the USA there was to be a special 2006 XK Victory Edition (the 'Victory' being to celebrate success in the North American Trans Am racing series).

Mechanically there were no important novelties built into the equipment of the 4.2S special edition, for the cars retained all the mechanical and same basic facelift visual package that had only recently been launched in 2004. Design director Ian Callum was, indeed, refreshingly honest about what was being done:

> Last year we made sure that the XK range was able to stand the test of time with a wide range of exterior design changes, such as a deeper mouth for the front air intake, new sills, and a revised rear bumper and spoiler. Now we have additional new colours and interior trims, to allow a customer to drive a Jaguar with a bespoke interior feel.

In fairness, apart from the introduction of yet another style of road wheel (the unique new 20in split-rim BBS Perseus item), the '4.2S' would really add no more, no less than that. There were also four new exterior metallic colours: Copper Black, Frost Blue, Bay Blue and Satin Silver, along with three interior colours, and two distinct veneer options for the instrument panel. From this point the XK8 was to have elm wood veneer as standard on the facia/instrument panel layout, while the XKR would have a sporty carbon-fibre veneer set. Special polished door tread-plates featured chequered flag emblems, and the same type of chequered flag motif featured on the revised 'Growler' badge at the front of the cars.

For sale only in the USA, the '2006 XK Victory Edition' cars were officially launched in April 2005. Strictly limited in volume – just over 1,000 would be manufactured – these paralleled the European '4.2S' types. To cele-

brate Jaguar's four Championship wins in the North American Trans Am road-racing series (by the way, these were with cars that might have looked like XKRs, but they had Ford-USA running gear and special chassis – which is why I have not covered them in this book!), they featured the same new body colour and interior novelties, along with the same new BBS wheels, and chequered-flag details on the 'growler' badges.

Now, as ever, this really was close to the end for the XK8. Already, in September 2004, Jaguar had announced that all final assembly at Browns Lane was to end in mid-2005, and although this decision was disputed by the trade unions for some months, it was finalized and formalized by the end of the calendar year. Although it was not spelt out at the time, this, and the launch of the advanced lightweight coupé concept in January 2005 (which presaged a move of sports car assembly to Browns Lane), indicated that the XK8/XKR was close to the end.

The launch of the two distinctly different (but closely related) 2005 special editions – '4.2S' and 'Victory' – helped boost demand in the last year. As is the way of things, too, once it became known that the car would soon be discontinued, there was a minor increase in sales. According to the production figures so kindly provided by Jaguar, no fewer than 4,007 cars were produced in 2005 – yet that was in a mere five months, a rate not previously approached by 4.2-litre cars, nor seen since 2001 when the original car's reputation was at its height.

The last XK8 car of all, carrying chassis number A48684, was built at Browns Lane on 27 May 2005, thus bringing to an end an unbroken sequence that had begun in 1951, when XK120 assembly had been moved over from the original factory at Foleshill.

Even so, the XK8 pedigree was not to be entirely lost, because over at Castle Bromwich, pilot production of the new-generation XK had already begun.

8 Replacing the XK8 – the New XK

As already noted, by 2004 the rumour-mongers were hard at it, forecasting the imminent death of the XK8, and changes that would be made for a new model. In an attempt to douse some of the speculation, Jaguar showed off the advanced lightweight coupé (ALC) show concept car in January 2005; but they kept many technical details under wraps, and would not say just how close to the specification of a new model the ALC actually was.

Even so, it wasn't until August 2005 that the first official details of a new production car were released: this was because the assembly machinery was still being installed, and initial deliveries were not planned until the first weeks of 2006. The new car was to abandon the 'XK8' title in favour of 'XK' instead, and although it looked very similar to the old XK8, the new car was almost entirely different.

At first glance, but only at first glance, the new XK might have been a careful re-skin of the ageing XK8, but even a few minutes' study of the two cars soon proved that this was not so. The fact that Jaguar had just closed down its

It was a huge compliment to the XK8 of 1996–2005 that its successor, the simply named XK, looked so similar. Although the structure was entirely different, the lines and general proportions were much as before.

When the all-new XK was being designed in the mid-2000s, Jaguar's staff looked at all details, from all angles, but the family resemblance was always obvious.

assembly lines at Browns Lane, and that the new XK was to be assembled alongside the technically radical XJ saloons at Castle Bromwich, was also important. Although the 4.2-litre AJ-V8 engine had been retained, albeit updated, virtually every other component was different. Behind the interest, not to say the hype, that surrounded the arrival of a new light-alloy body

From three-quarter rear, in 2005/2006, the new-generation XK was recognizably descended from the earlier car, even though every panel, and the structure, were novel, and the tail lamps were unique.

From this angle, can you tell the difference between the new XK and the successful XK8 that it replaced in 2005? No? What a compliment that really was!

In 2006, one way to pick the new-generation car from the earlier one was by noting the new profile of the head-lamp cowls, and the layouts of the projectors hidden away behind the glass.

shell, the adoption of different front and rear suspension architecture went almost unnoticed.

In fact, although the new car showed some superficial visual similarities to the XK8, it was based on an entirely new platform, and running gear that was closely related to the new-generation XJ saloons and to the contemporary S-Type, and no trace of the age-old XJS/XK8 'chassis' platform remained. On this occasion, visual design had been in the capable hands of Ian Callum, and, as with the XK8, there were to be hatchback coupé and convertible derivatives.

Jaguar made much of the claim that the new-type XK was all new, and instantly dispatched the elegant old XK8 to the 'obsolete' bin. Visually it wasn't exactly the same as the ALC had been, for there had been changes to the nose, the profile of the lights had changed, a rear hatchback (that the XK8 had always lacked) was now standardized, and there was a better looking and more aerodynamically efficient front 'splitter'. A new range – 18in, 19in or 20in diameter (instead of 21in) – of alloy wheels had been adopted, along with rounded instead of square-section exhaust tail pipes.

153

Every line, every detail and every styling theme of the new XK differed from that of the XK8 (and so it should, because the new car had been conceived a full decade after the original had taken shape). In some ways – but not in a way that Callum would ever advertise – some of the proportions and bulks of the new Jaguar were similar to those of the most recent Aston Martins – it being suggested that the two design teams had had access to each others' studios as the process advanced. Even so, Callum made the point that the new car's skin lines were more influenced by what they had to hide and to wrap around, than had been so with some earlier Jaguars: 'The XK must be inspired by Jaguar's heritage, but must never be beholden to it. I'm very confident about the car. It is sleek, elegant, powerful and athletic. A true Jaguar'.

Technicalities

Although the new car was almost exactly the same overall size as the old, it had a longer wheelbase, a more spacious cabin (the rear seats were almost usable by fully grown adults, instead of short-legged children, though leg room was still constrained), and it was a little lighter than before. Not only was this because the rather cramped old XJS/XK8 platform had finally been discarded, but there was also a new all-aluminium structure. This simple chart tells its own story:

Feature	New XK (2005)	Original XK8 of 1996
Wheelbase (in)	108.3	101.9
Overall length (in)	188.6	187.4
Engine size (cc)	4196	3996
Engine power (bhp)	295	290
Unladen weight (Coupé – lb)	3,517	3,557

The new structure was an all-aluminium assembly, with the platform having some similarities to the still new XJ saloons. Instead of the liberal use of robots and the ubiquitous welding gun, panels and structural members were fastened together by thousands of rivets, self-piercing screws and adhesives, but rarely by welding. Extruded alloy beams were used as key structural members in positions of high stress, including the door sills. Jaguar gleefully revealed a line of statistics confirming that each body shell would use 26,000 rivets of thirteen different designs, 90m of panel-to-panel adhesive, but a mere 0.5m of welding. It was suggested that if the production lines were to work flat out, then 13,134 new-type XKs could be built in every calendar year.

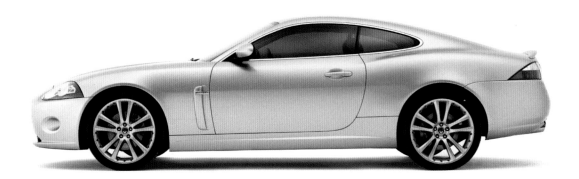

The new-generation XK of 2006 was very similar in general proportions to the 1996–2005 variety. Detail ways of picking the new from the old were by the layout of the front and rear lights, and by the positioning of the vertical cooling vent ahead of the doors. The use of a significantly longer wheelbase than before – the new car's wheelbase was 108.3in – was cleverly disguised.

As with the old-type XK8, so with the new-generation car, there were convertible and fixed-head coupé versions of the new design.

As with the XJ saloons, a number of complex alloy castings were fixed to critical points of the body shell (there were twenty-four of these in the coupé, twenty-two in the convertible), all of which helped to spread the loads and to provide mounting points for the suspension, engine and gearbox.

Clearly this all made the new XK's shell a more complex assembly than that of the outgoing XK8, but Jaguar claimed that, like for like, it was not only 20 per cent lighter than before, but torsionally extremely stiff – 16,000 Nm/degree for the convertible, and an astonishing 30,000Nm/degree for the hatchback

coupé. That, it was pointed out, made the convertible no less than 60 per cent more rigid than the XK8 had been.

By any standards, this was a remarkably advanced structure. It was one that Jaguar could surely never have contemplated developing, or spending capital sums on tooling for, if they had not been backed by Ford's massive resources. It was also understood that it forecast a long life for the new design, in order to achieve an acceptable investment 'payback'. To build this car, a series of new assembly lines were installed at the modern new plant developed at the Castle Bromwich factory, on the

The new-generation XKs had entirely different layouts of facia/instruments.

Without the huge backing and engineering expertise of Ford behind them, Jaguar might not have been able to bring forward this state-of-the-art navigation/instrumentation display as rapidly as it did.

eastern outskirts of Birmingham, where the new-generation XK would take shape alongside the XJ and S–Type ranges.

By comparison with the body shell itself, the running gear of the new car was positively familiar. The now-familiar 4.2-litre V8 engine, still to be manufactured at Ford's specialist engines plant at Bridgend in South Wales, had been worked over to meet the world's latest, and the latest proposed, exhaust emission standards, and would develop 295bhp in normally aspirated form, and a healthy 420bhp when supercharged.

When the car was launched there was also talk of adding the new, corporate, 205bhp/2.7-litre V6 diesel to the range (this Ford/Peugeot engine was already available in S–Type and XJ saloon ranges), but two years on there was still no sign of it ever coming to market. As on the

Although the new-type XK used the same basic six-speed ZF automatic transmission as before, there was a different 'J-gate' controlling the choice of ratios.

Compared with the XK8, the structure of the new-generation XK was very different, for much of the structure was in pressed and forged aluminium, bonded and riveted together. Although this was more complex than before, it was at once a lighter and stronger assembly.

XK8, all the available engines were backed by a ZF automatic transmission, but in this case it had been upgraded to the latest, fashionable six-speeder that was controlled by a combination of conventional change speed lever on the transmission tunnel, or by paddles placed behind the rim of the steering wheel. A manual transmission was not available.

Naturally, all-independent coil spring suspension was used, though there was nothing in

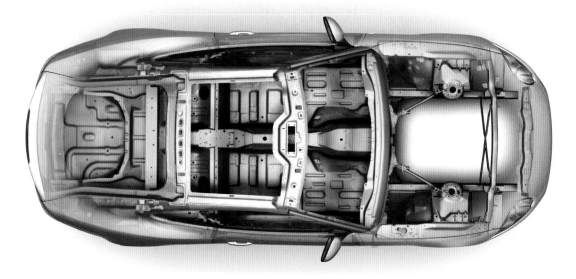

Like the XK8, which it replaced, the new-generation XK featured a rock-solid metal monocoque. The difference, in this case, was that much of the structure was in aluminium, rather than in pressed steel.

This was the front suspension of the new-type XK of 2006, different in every detail from that of the older car.

Like the XK8, its predecessor, the all-new XK of 2005 was astonishingly agile for such a big car.

In 2006, Jaguar issued this very clever montage, showing how the new-type XK was related to the successful XK8, and of course to the historic E-Type of earlier years.

common with the old XK8. At the front, an S-Type sub-frame and widely spread wish-bones made the i.f.s. look like a MacPherson system (though it was not!), while an XJ-type sub-frame, with wishbones, was used at the rear. Steering was by a power-assisted ZF rack-and-pinion system, telescopic dampers were computer-sensed, and there were four huge brake discs to keep the whole thing in check.

When the car went on sale in the first weeks of 2006, a UK domestic market comparison of prices between the last of the XK8s and the first new-generation XK was interesting:

Model	Outgoing XK8	New XK
Coupé	£51,195	£59,000
Convertible	£57,995	£65,000

The new car, in other words, was 15 per cent (Coupé/Hatchback) or 12 per cent (Convertible) more costly than before, but Jaguar hoped that the technical advances and the up-to-the-minute style of the new car would justify this. Jaguar's accountants, of course, would presumably not be happy until sales exceeded the 90,616 total of the long-running XK8.

Appendix:
Blood Relation –
the Aston Martin DB7

It all began over a drink in Italy in 1987. Ford's Walter Hayes had joined veteran journalist Gordon Wilkins's house party in Bergamo, assembled to enjoy themselves prior to the revived Mille Miglia event, and had met up with Aston Martin's then chairman Victor Gauntlett. As ever, the extrovert chairman was too cash-strapped to contemplate major new model programmes, and it was during this weekend that he confirmed that this famous, but loss-making, old British company could be available for sale.

After Hayes returned to England, he contacted Ford's Henry Ford II, suggested that the company should be bought, and saw the job done before the end of the year. That, as far as Hayes was concerned, should have been that. But shortly after he retired from Ford (he had

Styled by a different hand, but sharing the same basic platform and layout of the running gear, the Aston Martin DB7 was previewed in 1993 and went on sale in 1994. This was the Volante (the company's name for a soft-top car) of the later 1990s.

The supercharged derivative of the Jaguar AJ16 engine, shown here in its XJR application, was used to power the DB7. Although this was briefly considered for the XK8 application too, it was to be discarded in favour of the all-new V8 instead.

Much of the flavour of the Aston Martin DB7's facia/instrument panel was similar to that of the XK8 that would follow two years later.

Which do you find prettier: this car, the Aston Martin DB7, or the Jaguar XK8, which was its kissing cousin? Don't forget that the DB7 was considerably more costly, and panelled in aluminium.

reached his sixty-fifth birthday in 1989, when corporate regulations brought down the axe), he was then invited to join the board of Aston Martin; he soon became its executive chairman, and discovered that the company's new model cupboard was almost bare – and decided to do something about it.

Reviving such an 'olde worlde' company, where no more than a handful of cars was being completed every week, and where the word 'profit' was unfamiliar to anyone in the management hierarchy, was going to be difficult. Before Hayes arrived, others had tried, and all had failed. This time, though, Hayes-the-fixer and Hayes-the-guru was not about to be denied. Encouraged by no less than HFII himself, and after showing a healthy disregard for the foot-dragging traditionalists who did

not want to see *any* new type of Aston Martin go on sale, Hayes set out on a new track.

Using every ounce of the formidable influence that he still enjoyed in the Ford empire, Hayes soon homed in on the existing Jaguar XJS platform and running gear, took a long look at the Jaguar XJ41 project that Ford had recently cancelled – and elected to start all over again. At this point, every trace of a stillborn 'small Aston Martin' project coded DP1999 was obliterated. Previous and rather tentative attempts to develop this new and 'cheaper' Aston Martin were indeed examined, but soon ruthlessly cast aside. Each and every one of those projects had taken shape around an all-new platform and chassis (which meant that investment would have been costly, and the development programme long), but Hayes

A straight race in more than one way! For the James Bond film of 2002, Die Another Day, *James Bond ran a specially modified silver Aston Martin Vanquish (which had supplanted the DB7), while his deadly rival used a dark green Jaguar XKR.*

How would you have liked to see a 450bhp/6-litre/V12-engined Jaguar XKR? Physically it was possible, because this Cosworth-manufactured V12 was fitted to the Aston Martin DB7 Vantage from the mid-1990s.

Ian Callum was the design/styling chief who produced the DB7 models in the early 1990s, and would later move over to Jaguar to take responsibility for the ever-evolving Jaguar XK8 models.

discarded that philosophy at once. Spurred on by his unmatchable connections, he decided to persist in his interest in the XJS platform and running gear, and set his staff to work.

Even so, the kernel of a new car had been conceived elsewhere, outside Aston Martin. Tom Walkinshaw's TWR conglomerate had set up the JaguarSport subsidiary during the 1980s, and had gone on to produce hundreds of faster and more extrovertly styled versions of the XJ-S and other models. With the ambitious mid-engined XJ220 launched, and in preparation at the Wykham Mill factory in Bloxham, near Banbury, JaguarSport then turned to another Jaguar-based project.

The unimaginatively coded 'XX' project took shape around a modified Jaguar XJ41 platform, and was intended to be powered by a detuned, road-going version of the TWR racing version of the Jaguar V12 power unit, complete with 4-valve/twin-cam cylinder heads. After hiring Ian Callum to develop its

165

own styling studios, JaguarSport/TWR tried to interest Jaguar's new owners, Ford, in having the car put into production; but with the XJ41 now cancelled, they never got very far with that proposal, even when a second proposal was to have it powered by a twin turbocharged Jaguar AJ6 6-cylinder engine.

With other commercial pressures taking up much more of their attention at Jaguar, Ford swiftly lost interest in that car, but soon afterwards Hayes concluded that the only way for him to get speedy approval for a new Aston Martin was to use this JaguarSport/TWR/Jaguar project as a basis, to start up a new project dubbed NPX (Newport Pagnell Experimental) and to commission a fresh two-door body style, closely related to that of the XX. Accordingly, it was absolutely no coincidence that the shape eventually chosen for the DB7 was very similar to that of the Project XX style (Ian Callum had been responsible for both), and even to the XK8 that would follow it.

Working at a whirlwind pace, but in his usual suave, logical and utterly persuasive manner, Hayes soon gained corporate approval for the new car to be developed, and set up a new company, called Aston Martin Oxford, with Walkinshaw; this meant that the new model could be totally engineered, styled and prototyped away from Aston Martin's Newport Pagnell HQ. The work could all be done in one corner of the sprawling TWR complex in Kidlington, just north of Oxford: that facility had matured during the engineering of the Jaguar XJ220 supercar project, so it was already well known to top management at Jaguar. With work beginning in 1991, the existence of NPX was publicly revealed in 1992, and the new car – it would come to be known as an Aston Martin DB7 – was officially unveiled (a full year before production could begin) in March 1993. Sales began in the autumn of 1994.

As with the XX, Ian Callum was also chosen to shape the new Aston Martin, to a brief from Hayes that was very carefully, but succinctly, defined. As Walter Hayes admitted at the time: 'We photographed the most beautiful DB4s and DB6s we could find, stuck the pictures up in the studio, and said: "Like that"….'

Callum, of course, did much better than 'like that' and later commented about the new DB7:

I wanted to keep it as low as possible, but we already had the package established so mandatory items determined much of the car. Anyway, I'm of the belief that styling should not hide the parameters of the package – a car should look like the car it's meant to be.

The shape of the new two-plus-two coupé model – originally coded NPX (for Newport Pagnell Experimental) – speaks for itself, while the running gear – hidden away under a sleek envelope with no exterior panels, in common with the XK8 that would follow – was much more familiar. The engine, transmission and suspension – the 'oily bits' – were all closely related to that of the XJS (which means that the platform and suspension, if not the actual power train, would eventually be related to the XK8, too) and therefore deserves this analysis.

Although the DB7's engine/transmission were closely related to those of the XJS, they were not lifted straight out of the cancelled XJ41. That car was to have had a twin-turbo 4-litre derivative version of the 24-valve, 6-cylinder AJ6 engine, whereas the DB7 would have a supercharged version of the smaller, 3.2-litre derivative. Nor, for that matter, would the running gear share anything of the forthcoming XK8, which was to take shape around the brand new V8 engine.

As finalized for the NPX/DB7, the Eaton-supercharged AJ6-type straight-six of 3239cc developed 335bhp at 5,750rpm, while there was to be a choice of five-speed Getrag manual or four-speed ZF automatic transmission. Even so, this was enough to provide the DB7 with a top speed of 157mph (251km/h). Incidentally, a 6-cylinder-engined DB7 weighed 3,795lb/1,725kg, significantly more than the equivalent XK8 (admittedly with a V8 engine), which weighed 3,557lb/1,615kg.

Although Aston Martin was originally coy about the origins of the DB7 platform and underpinnings (they never categorically denied that it was based on that of the XJS, but they never actually confirmed it either, and in later years they always tried studiously to ignore any references to the heritage of the platform!), the fact is that, except in detail, the platform, the wheelbase and track dimensions, the front and rear suspension and steering, were all closely related to those of the XJS – and, by definition, were also closely related to what would soon be used out of sight, under the skin of the new XK8.

Aston Martin DB7: How Much XJS and XK8 Under the Skin?

This is not something that Aston Martin *or* Jaguar publicists are totally happy to talk about – at least in detail. If you looked carefully under the skin of the Aston Martin DB7, which went on sale during 1994, you would find an amazing amount of familiar Jaguar XJS (later XK8) hardware – not just the bare bones of the engine, but the transmission, the suspension and the modified platform, too.

In fact this is a simple little story, the connection of course being Ford. The American giant took control of Aston Martin at the end of 1987, and of Jaguar in 1989, and it was soon obvious that a degree of rationalization might be appropriate. Soon after Ford appointed its distinguished elder statesman, Walter Hayes, to be Aston Martin's Chairman, work on a new Aston Martin model began in earnest.

Time to step back a pace. Jaguar had spent time in the 1980s designing and developing the XJ41 sports coupé, whose aim in life was to take over from the XJS. The XJ41, however, was cancelled soon after Ford took control, the prototypes being banished, to sit under dust sheets in Jaguar's design centre at Whitley.

In the meantime Walter Hayes set up Aston Martin Oxford with Tom Walkinshaw's TWR Group, and work was started on a Jaguar-based 'XX' car in 1991. The Aston Martin NPX (Newport Pagnell Experimental) followed in 1992. From the beginning, the plan was for Aston Martin Oxford to engineer the car, and for it to be produced at the JaguarSport factory at Bloxham, near Banbury, just as soon as assembly of Jaguar XJ220s (which were built there) had ceased.

Prototypes of the DB7, in fact, were unveiled in March 1993, well before deliveries could begin, the first customer cars actually not leaving Bloxham until the summer of 1994, priced at £78,500. The DB7's fastback coupé style was by Ian Callum of TWR, and, to quote Walter Hayes: 'We photographed the most beautiful DB4s and DB6s we could find, stuck the pictures up in the studio, and said "Like that"....' Those 'in the know' say that the DB7 looks rather like the final, cancelled XJ41, which may be true, but in any case it now stands on its own as a beautiful machine.

Although Aston Martin spokesmen always insisted that the DB7 used a unique pressed platform, no production engineer ever took such a claim seriously. There is no doubt that it used a modified and updated version of the XJS layout, with identical wheelbase and slightly wider track dimensions (which became the XK8 layout in the late 1990s). The suspension layouts – most noticeably the independent rear suspension, complete with its massive pressed bridge supporting the axle, springs, dampers and pivots – were clearly Jaguar-derived.

The DB7's engine was a modified version of the Jaguar AJ16 3.2-litre, complete with an Eaton supercharger (Eaton's blower would be used on supercharged Jaguar saloons, and the XKR, later in the decade), and produced 335bhp at 5,500rpm. When the car went on sale in 1994 this compared with the 241bhp, normally aspirated Jaguar 3.2-litre in the XJS, and with the 321bhp Eaton-supercharged 4-litre types fitted to the new-generation XJ6 saloons.

Behind the engine there was a choice of Getrag five-speed all-synchromesh, or ZF 4HP22 four-speed automatic transmissions, these also being the transmissions then being used in the 6-cylinder-engined XJS.

So, what if it was really a Jaguar XJS under a stylish new body? To quote the *Autocar* road test of the DB7 in October 1994:

It is no coincidence that the DB7 shares engine and suspension designs with the Jaguar XJS. Deep, deep in its history, it *is* an XJS.... Aston Martin has never commented on the DB7's tortured genesis, and nor need it. It only knows how badly it needed NPX, Jag-based or not.

Although the Aston DB7 Volante looked similar to the XK8 in general proportions, the body shells were different in every detail.

When the new V12 engine was fitted to the Aston Martin DB7, thus creating the Vantage, there was no change to the style, which remained eerily close to that of the Jaguar XK8.

The Aston Martin DB7 and DB7 Vantage models resembled the Jaguar XK8 in so many ways – including the choice of closed coupé, or drop head coupé (Volante) types.

Mass production, by Aston Martin standards. Aston Martin built their 4,000th DB7 at the Bloxham Mill factory, near Banbury, in February 2001. Each and every one of those cars used the same basic platform as that of the XJS, which also provided the grounding for the XK8, too.

Assembly of the DB7

By comparison with the XJS (and the XK8 that followed), assembly of the DB7 was a tortuous business. Pressed-steel platform assemblies and inner panels (basically XJS items) were produced at Jaguar's body plant at Castle Bromwich, on the eastern outskirts of Birmingham, before being delivered to the independent concern, Mayflower Vehicles Systems (previously known as Motor Panels), in Coventry, where the balance of the body shell was completed. Much of this assembly was zinc-coated steel, but the bonnet, front wings, impact-absorbing bumper, end panels, removable roof panels, sills and the boot lid were all moulded in composite materials produced by one of Tom Walkinshaw's advanced technology subsidiaries.

Once complete, in the first two years the shells were then transported to Rolls-Royce at Crewe, where they were treated to that company's renowned anti-corrosion treatment and its careful painting operation. It was not until the late 1990s that a new paint shop was completed at Bloxham, after which this operation was taken back 'in house'.

Once the body shell was painted and ready, finally assembly of all DB7s took place at Bloxham. It was significant, in so many ways, that Bloxham had always been the home of Jaguar's extraordinary XJ220 'Supercar' project, whose body shells were also produced by Motor Panels – these two interlinked facts meant that the building of DB7s could not begin until the last XJ220s had been completed.

In the meantime, modified Jaguar-type engines were completed at a TWR facility (TWR Engines) in Kidlington, north of Oxford, where the German-sourced transmissions, manual or automatic, were mated to those engines before they were trucked to Bloxham for final assembly.

Very few DB7s would be completed in 1994 (a fire on *Autocar*'s launch car, found to be a production fault concerning exhaust pipe alignment, set things back for a couple of months): assembly did not begin until June 1994, and for the first months only one car was being completed, and signed off, every week.

When Aston Martin added the Vanquish to its range in 2001, there were no mechanical links to the Jaguar XK8, but the style still owed much to that car's lines.

Even so, with the company finally satisfied with the quality of the series-production DB7s, more than 700 followed in 1995, and investment at Bloxham finally pushed up the ultimate capacity to 1,500 cars per year, though this output was never achieved.

Before long there was a drop-head coupé Vantage too, and from 1999 Aston Martin would introduce a 6-litre V12-engined version. The very first V12-engined car was built in 1996 as a one-off for Tom Walkinshaw to use, this particular car being powered by a 6.4-litre/twin-cam/48-valve version of the Jaguar/TWR engine set to produce 475bhp and deliver up to 182mph (293km/h).

Ford and Jaguar, however, did not want this ancient (though superbly modernized) V12 engine to be used in a production car – it had already been withdrawn from main-stream Jaguars, and the manufacturing machine at Radford was being removed – so instead the company was guided in the direction of a brand new, Ford-sponsored 6-litre V12. This power unit, an evolution of the 60-degree V6/3-litre to be found in cars such as the latest Mondeo, was carefully and resourcefully finalized by Cosworth (also a Ford subsidiary at the time), and was put into small, but nevertheless series production at Cosworth's road-cars assembly plant at Wellingborough. With 420bhp at first, and 435bhp on later derivatives of these cars, this engine propelled the DB7 V12 to 185mph (298km/h), which could match any Ferrari of the period.

From the three-quarter rear view, the Aston Martin Vanquish of 2001 looks similar to the XK8 in so many ways.

By the early 2000s, Aston Martin had also commissioned various limited-edition models, Zagato-modified derivatives, and even a Zagato-bodied open car, the DBAR ('AR' meaning 'American Roadster'), although even those cars retained the same basic XJS/XK8 platform and suspension layouts.

DB7 Production

More than 7,000 DB7s of all types were eventually produced, which represented one in three of all Aston Martins so far manufactured since the company was founded! The last of all was built at Bloxham just before the end of 2003, and this car was immediately put in the BMIHT museum at Gaydon. The last DB7-derived cars of all were the American Roadsters, which Zagato completed in Italy in 2004. At that point, all Aston Martin's physical links with Jaguar, the XJS and the XK8 were lost, as future Aston Martins had a unique architecture all of their own.

For the record, DB7 production of each model was as follows:

DB7 6-cylinder (including 879 Volante Convertibles)	2,449
DB7 V12-cylinder (Coupé and Volante) (including 190 DB7 GT and 112 DB7 GTA)	4,444
DB7 Zagato Coupé	99
DBAR (American Roadster/ Zagato shell)	99
Grand total	7,091

Index